Acknowledgements and Thanks

Try Vegan PDX is very happy to be presenting our second annual Try Vegan Week in 2009. It is quite an undertaking to put on over 20 events during the course of one week. Many people have helped us out along the way, either by volunteering their time to plan or present an event during the week, contribute content to our guidebook, mentor new vegans or donate space for our many classes, workshops and lectures.

The following people have made Try Vegan Week and The Vegan Guide to Portland a reality for a second year in a row: David Agranoff, Deanna Cintas, Heather Morgan, Tina Lamanna, Megan Brooker, Randall Perez, Jessica DeNoto, Chelsea Lincoln, Valerie Ambrose, Chris Emery, Ren Fox, Elizabeth Miller, Brian Heck, Liene Verzemnieks, Ed Bauer, John Lovell, Nick Young and Joshua Wold.

Introduction

Portland is a wonderful place to live or visit. Portlanders who choose the eco- and animal-friendly lifestyle of veganism are lucky to call this city home. Known as one of the most vegan-friendly communities on the planet, Portland has amazing food options and unique grassroots resources..

It is easy to point out the foods: amazing downtown eateries with cheap raw food dishes, a 24-hour-a-day donut shop with vegan donuts, $1.00 homemade vegan corn dog nights, a gourmet all-vegan Italian restaurant, 17" pancakes and, of course, the world's only all-vegan mini-mall.

Those are some of the many attractions that make Portland a great destination for a vegan vacation. The vegan community holds many events, ranging from our annual VegFest, free classes, free year-round vegan mentoring, social activities, and a vegan medical clinic.

This guidebook has three uses. For Portland residents who are new to or considering veganism, it can serve as a guide to the world of options they may not have been aware existed. We have discovered that even long-time vegans often miss some of the cool things that are available.

For vegans in other cities, we hope you will use this book to plan a stop in Portland on your next vacation. You can use this guide to read about all the options available if you choose to visit.

Last but certainly not least, we have noticed that Portland's vegan-friendliness has caused an influx: Vegans from all over the country are moving to Portland. We welcome you; the more vegans, the stronger our community will be. So we hope vegans considering a move to Portland can use this book to learn more about their new or future home.

Being vegan feels great. More importantly, this simple and meaningful change in diet will spare some of the billions of animals who suffer daily. Committing yourself to a vegan diet shows compassion for animals and concern for the environment with every bite. We hope this guide will serve as a companion to our mentoring program, because as an organization our mission is to help anyone who is interested learn just how easy, healthy, and enjoyable a vegan life in Portland can be.

Table of Contents

Frequently Asked Questions

Q: What does vegan mean? What is a vegan?

A: A vegan is someone who consumes no animal products, including flesh foods, dairy products, or eggs. Vegans also refrain from using animal products in non-food capacities like leather shoes.

Q: Why would I want to do that?

A: There are lots of reasons to go vegan! Many people are inspired to give up animal products when they learn about the atrocities committed against farm animals. Adopting a vegan diet is a refusal to participate in that system of feedlots and de-beaking. Environmental concerns are another reason why many people choose a vegan lifestyle.   A number of reports have been released recently that compare the environmental effects of eating meat with those of driving: Producing one pound of meat emits the same amount of greenhouse gases as driving an SUV forty miles. If animal products' negative effects on the animals and on are planet aren't enough to convince you, consider your own health: Vegans are less likely to suffer from common illnesses like cancer, heart disease, diabetes, and osteoporosis.

Q: How can a vegan diet be healthy?   Isn't it lacking in nutrients?

A: A well-planned vegan diet contains more fruits and vegetables, more fiber, and less saturated fat than the typical American diet, and since cholesterol comes only from animal sources, a vegan diet is automatically cholesterol-free.

While there is no nutrient that cannot be obtained from a vegan diet, it's true that vegans need to pay special attention to ensure adequate levels of some of them. Vitamin B12, which generally only occurs in animal products, is perhaps the most crucial. However, nutritional yeast, a favorite vegan condiment/ingredient, contains high levels of B12. Many foods, such as cereals, soy milk, and meat analogs, are supplemented with B12. Those who are still concerned can take a supplement.

Calcium is another nutrient that vegans might be worried about. The dairy industry would have us believe that milk is the only source of calcium in the world, but that couldn't be farther from the truth. In fact, leafy green vegetables, tofu, and fortified soy milks are some of the many sources of calcium in a vegan diet.

Vegans also need to pay attention to vitamin D. Vitamin D is rarely found naturally in foods; your skin produces all you need with exposure to sunlight. In the summer, all you need to do to maintain adequate levels is to spend a few minutes outside without sunscreen. In the winter, however, Portland's latitude makes it impossible to get enough sun for proper vitamin D production. Most dairy products are fortified with vitamin D, so milk-drinkers can make up that deficit without even thinking about it. Vegans, however, should consider taking a supplement during the winter. Keep in mind that vitamin D3 (cholecalciferol), the form that is in most supplements and many fortified foods, is not vegan. Vitamin D2 (ergocalciferol) is vegan, and is often sold as "Dry Vitamin D" tablets.

It does need to be said that it is entirely possible to eat an unhealthy vegan diet. After all, french fries and SweetPea cupcakes are vegan, but trying to live off of only those foods would not be a great choice for health! However, with just a bit of thought it is not very difficult to plan a vegan diet that is far healthier than an omnivorous one.

Q: But where do you get your protein?

A: That is the question that might, one day, make some poor vegan's head explode. Here's the thing: The average American eats far more protein--twice as much, according to some estimates--than he needs. So while vegans might not eat as much protein as someone following a traditional meat-and-potatoes diet, they can still get all the protein they need easily. Here's another thing: Almost every food contains some protein. It is virtually impossible to eat a varied, calorically-adequate diet without getting enough protein. But if you're still worried, try eating tofu, beans, nuts, quinoa, nut butters, seitan, hummus, tempeh, lentils...

Q: What's the point of avoiding milk and eggs? Taking those doesn't kill the cow or the chicken, so what's the problem?

A: There are a lot of problems, actually. The egg and dairy industries are notoriously cruel, to the point that some committed vegans believe that eating meat but avoiding eggs and dairy is a more compassionate choice than ovo-lacto-vegetarianism. At least, the argument goes, once they slaughter an animal for meat its suffering ends; chickens and dairy cows might be tortured for years. (Try Vegan PDX believes, of course, that avoiding *all* animal products is the only truly compassionate choice.)

Dairy cows are typically kept constantly pregnant, then separated from their offspring, which causes visible distress to both cow and calf. Many of the calves end up in veal crates, a practice whose cruelty shocks even dedicated meat-eaters. Meanwhile, the cows are treated less like living, feeling creatures than as milk-production equipment. They are hooked up to milking machines that often cause painful irritations and infections to their teats, and are forced to produce several times more milk per day than they would naturally. When they are no longer "productive," they are slaughtered. And they are forced to live out most of this unnaturally-shortened life inside a crowded milking shed with little or no access to the outdoors.

Egg production is just as sad. Laying hens are usually confined to a cage too small for them to spread their wings or turn around. Many hens resort to pecking themselves or others as a way to deal with the stress of living in such conditions; production facilities typically solve that problem not by improving conditions to reduce stress, but by searing off hens' beaks to prevent pecking. Battery hens are bred and manipulated to lay up to 300 times more eggs than they would naturally, and are killed when they can no longer produce at that rate.

Since we've already established that it is possible to live a healthy life without supporting those sorts of practices, why should compassionate, thinking, informed people contribute to an industry that causes such suffering?

Q: But I only buy cage-free or free-range eggs and organic milk, so that's OK, right?

A: Well, maybe. Or maybe not. The problem is, there's very little regulation as to what those terms really mean. "Cage-free" hens might have a little more space than battery hens, or they might be crammed in just as tightly, only without cages. They still might be de-beaked. And they are still killed after their productive egg-laying months, a small fraction of their natural lifespan, are over. Organic dairy products might still come from cows who have spent most of their lives in confinement, thanks to loopholes in the organic standards and agri-businesses who jump at the chance to exploit them.

Q: What about honey?

A: Good question! Honey is sometimes seen as something of a gray area; many vegans avoid it, but some do not. However, honey is produced by bees, as an ideal food source for a bee's nutritional needs. The sugar-water solution that many commercial beekeepers replace it with (after helping themselves to the fruits of the bees' labor) is inadequate. Commercial beekeepers also often kill queen bees every year or two as a way to maintain their control over the hive. These practices point to the abuse and exploitation of bees, who are animals as important as any other; therefore, honey is not a part of a vegan diet.

Q: Besides diet, what do vegans need to consider?

A: Vegans avoid animal products in all forms. That includes clothing, accessories, furniture, etc. made from leather, wool, silk, and other animal-produced materials. You might also be surprised at the number of animal by-products that turn up in common personal-care products such as lotions, soaps, and make-up. Vegans check ingredient labels on those sorts of products carefully, and also avoid any that have been tested on animals. Some, but not all, vegans also consider the ownership of the corporations that manufacture products. For example, if a company that makes soy milk is owned by a parent company that also produces dairy milk, some people might consider that brand of soy milk non-vegan regardless of its ingredients.

Q: How can you live your life while worrying about all that?

A: It seems really overwhelming at first, but over time it honestly does become habit, then second-nature. Also keep in mind that there is no vegan police; no one will throw you out of the club if you forget to check a label and buy a wool-blend sweater. The fact is, animal products are so widespread throughout our culture that there is no such thing as a "perfect" vegan. For example, almost all tires are made with animal products. But even knowing that, vegans still need to get places, so we replace the tires on our cars and bikes, or pay fares to transit agencies that spend our money on new bus tires. The point is, individuals must decide for themselves just how vegan they're willing and able to be, and do their best to meet those standards. This isn't permission to eat a hunk of bacon and still call yourself vegan, but rather an acknowledgment that we all practice veganism to the best of our abilities, and we all mess up occasionally. When it happens, please be as compassionate to yourself as you are toward the animals.

Shopping for the Vegan Kitchen

Portland vegans have myriad options for stocking their kitchens, so let's explore some of the possibilities. Some sources are good for finding close-out bargains, others are essential for your organic produce needs, and still others are havens for vegan specialty products. The Try Vegan PDX gang believes in supporting local and vegan-friendly businesses whenever possible; however, sometimes we just need to get stuff on the cheap! Developing vegan-friendly shopping habits may seem daunting at first, but you will soon adapt and get to know Portland's vegan resources.

Store tours with an experienced vegan mentor are always available by appointment by contacting www.tryveganpdx.com

* Places to shop:

Small specialty stores and ethnic groceries, big-name chain stores, close-out discount stores, on-line retailers, farmers' markets, co-ops and CSAs can all be great sources for things we need. You can find these sorts of stores anywhere you go by checking websites like happycow.net and vegdining.com, contacting local vegetarian groups, or even looking in the good old-fashioned phone book. Here in Portland, we recommend:

1. Specialty stores and ethnic groceries: Asian and other specialty markets, which are plentiful in Portland, are great places to stock up on hard-to-find items or to get a great deal on common ones. Here are some TVPDX favorites:

~Food Fight! Grocery, SE 12th and Stark - Holy shizzle! This is Portland's 100%, no BS vegan grocery. Here you'll find all of the awesome vegan treats you could ever imagine, along with a great selection of vegan groceries, health and beauty items, cruelty-free cleaning products, stuff for your dog and cat, and many yummy meat and dairy analogs. Stock up on locally-made candy bars, vegan marshmallows, vegan cheeses, ice creams, mock fish and crab, chocolate gift boxes, cookbooks, and more! If that isn't enough, Food Fight! also has a decent selection of organic produce and items like organic grains, nutritional yeast and flours in bulk. We think you will love this place. *Note: while some of the prices here may seem high, remember as a small store, Food Fight! can only buy products in small quantities, unlike much larger chain stores. The bonus is that

when we shop here, we are supporting a vegan store owned by people who sincerely care about animals. Food Fight! also supports activist groups with frequent donations. Come here for organic produce, bulk foods, and lip balm, and put together a great care package for your Aunt Nellie in Arkansas, who has no access to awesome vegan treats! Don't live in Portland? Go on-line to shop www.foodfightgrocery.com and have your stuff mailed to your door!

~*Fubonn Asian shopping center, SE 82nd, between Division St. and Powell Blvd.* - The large grocery store at its center is the best reason to visit this Asian mall. It is an Asian food super store with all kinds of analogs, noodles, spices, curry pastes, teas, and anything else you can imagine--and plenty of stuff you can't! While this store definitely deserves a visit, it is large and can get crowded and overwhelming. We think that the smaller Asian markets offer a more pleasant, low-key experience with nearly the same selection of products.

~*An Dong, SE 54th and Powell Blvd.* - A small, family-owned Asian market, An Dong has a very good selection of vegan products with decent prices. Go there for inexpensive teas, locally-made organic tofu, mock fish, all kinds of unusual hot sauces and chili pastes, cooking oils, goji berries, canned gluten products, Thai curries, noodles, herbs, dried mushrooms, fresh Asian vegetables and fruits, sea vegetables, spices and much more. One caveat is that An Dong does have a large animal flesh department, which may be hard to avoid seeing.

~*Limbo produce market, SE 39th, near Holgate (next to Trader Joe's)* - Oh, Limbo, how we love thee! This is a great place for all of your fresh, organic produce needs. Load up your backpack with organic broccoli, avocados, yams, greens, garlic, grapes and strawberries. Besides the produce, Limbo is known for their "wall of herbs:" floor-to-ceiling jars of bulk medicinal and culinary herbs, teas, and spices. They also carry almost the full line of Bob's Red Mill products, local breads, and essential oils. You can get nearly everything you need by shopping at Limbo for fresh produce and the Trader Joe's next door for other grocery items.

~*India 4 You, SE Belmont @ 36th Ave* - Indian specialty market. Get your Indian groceries here, as well as homemade samosas and other yummy Indian treats!

~*Other* - There are other ethnic and specialty markets scattered around Portland. African, Central American, and Middle Eastern markets all have specialty vegan products!

2. Co-ops -

~People's - SE 21st, one block north of Powell Blvd. - A fixture in southeast since 1970, People's Co-op is a small-but-loaded store that is 100% vegetarian. Visit their farmers' market (not flesh-free) on Wednesdays, and get a fresh juice or smoothie at the Sip juice cart outside. Shop here for the incredible selection of bulk items, including tofu, vegan cream cheese, hummus, seitan, Stonewall's soy jerky, pastas, grains, oils, vinegars, nuts, and much more. Also in bulk: dish and laundry soaps, cat and dog foods, lotions, and shampoo. You may never have to buy anything in packaging again!

~Alberta Street Co-op, NE Alberta St. - Small, but packed with stuff; lots of bulk.

~Food Front, NW Thurman & 24th, SW Capitol Hwy. - Portland's oldest co-op has everything you need, including a good selection of organic produce, pantry staples, and lots of bulk. Check out their deli, which offers a great selection of prepared foods (not all vegan) including favorites like the faux chicken salad.

3. Chain stores -

~Whole Foods, Pearl District, Laurelhurst, Beaumont (Northeast), and coming soon to Hollywood District - Giant "natural foods" grocery. Plenty of vegan stuff to tempt you, but be prepared to pay more for processed, packaged items. Good bulk section, good prices on their own "365" brand of staple items such as canned organic beans & veggies, soy milks, and certain frozen items. Excellent selection of supplements and health & beauty products.

~New Seasons, various locations all over Portland - Locally-owned, mostly "natural foods" grocery that will leave your wallet crying in pain. While this is a good place to find some items, it tends to be expensive. Go there for a good selection of supplements, bulk foods, organic produce and vegan grocery items.

~Trader Joe's, NE 42nd & Halsey, NW 21st & Glisan, and SE 39th & Holgate - There's a lot to be said for Trader Joe's. In case you don't know, TJ's thing is to acquire the right to sell specially-selected brand-name products, put their own labels on them, and sell the products for less. They carry an impressive selection of vegan products, and have even started labeling many vegan products with a "V" logo. Stock up on reasonably-priced organic canned goods, salad dressings and other condiments, pastas, prepared meals, snacks, frozen organic veggies and fruits, breakfast items, organic salads, vegan milks, bread, and lots of other stuff. You'll find some inexpensive, high-end type stuff that you may not be able to afford in other stores. Good place for those on a budget.

~The big chain groceries - Many now carry a pretty good selection of vegan and organic products. Safeway, Fred Meyer, and Zupan's all have food vegans eat. Fred Meyer now has its own health food section, as well as some organic produce and bulk items. Safeway markets its "O" brand of organic products to those looking for more healthful options. While Zupan's does carry plenty of vegan stuff, be prepared to pay up, because they are not cheap.

4. Discount Stores -

The two with the best selection are *Big Lots, Mall 205* location, and *Grocery Outlet, Hollywood District and Gresham.* Big Lots can be hit or miss, but often they have super cheap food items. Check there frequently, as they get new stuff weekly.

Grocery Outlet is a reliable place for discounted vegan products. Their selection also changes frequently, but it's common to find frozen vegan meals, natural-foods cereals, chips and snacks, and random awesome finds like vegan pesto, veggie burgers and other analogs, soy and rice milks, teas, produce, and cheap cruelty-free shampoos, lotion, toothpaste, and the like. Go to Grocery Outlet if you're on a budget. They always have a good selection, and you just might walk away with an amazing, super-cheap find.

5. Farmer's markets and CSAs -

Almost every neighborhood in Portland hosts a farmers' market, and there is a large one every Saturday on the campus of Portland State University, in Southwest Portland. Great deals are always to be had when you cut out the middle people and buy directly from the people who grow the food. For more details, visit their website: www.portlandfarmersmarket.org

*Checking Ingredients:

If you are a novice when it comes to recognizing animal ingredients on labels, have no shame; we were all there once. Refer to the Animal Ingredients A-Z Guide in this book to familiarize yourself with potential non-vegan ingredients. One important thing to remember is that unless you already know that something is vegan, or unless the product says *Vegan* on the label--as many now do--you should read every label to be sure.

Reading labels is not the hassle you might think it is, and it gets easier and eventually becomes second nature. Here are some common "WTF?" ingredients you'll need to look out for: whey, casein, sodium casinate (dairy), albumen (egg), stearic acid & sterol (can be either veg or animal-derived), mono- and/or di-glycerides (can be either veg or animal-derived) "natural flavoring" (can be anything), and carmine (red coloring agent that comes from a beetle). If you're unsure of the origin of an ingredient, you might want to call the company before making the purchase. Every food manufacturer has a consumer information number which is usually listed on the product's label.

*Finding the good stuff

Which products are good? Which ones are not so good? We've all tried a product like a vegan cheese or milk which was not so good. The fact is, there are tasty, amazing analogs and other vegan products available, but how do we know which ones to get? The best way to do this if you are a new vegan, is to consult with an old vegan!

Contact Try Vegan PDX for a store tour, or hang out with one of our mentors for a while until you feel confident about your product choices. No one likes to get something that sounded yummy, only to find that it totally stinks. Trial and error will also be necessary to some degree, especially since individual tastes vary. New products come out all the time, and in Portland it doesn't take long for word to get around about whether a product is good or bad. Also, the peeps at Food Fight! Grocery will be happy to tell you about the best vegan products.

Lastly, do not expect the vegan stuff to taste like the animal products you've been used to. Your tastes will adapt, though, and over time you will either forget the difference, or ask yourself why you ever liked those animal products in the first place. The thought of them will likely gross you out. This is the common vegan experience. You'll likely find yourself thinking: "Eewww, amniotic fluid sacs!" or "Nasty! Cow mucus and fat!"

*Types of foods

~Produce -

What can we say except, eat more of it! If you have not been a big fresh produce eater, you need to start. This is where disease prevention and optimal wellness happen. Get some damned cookbooks (or raw books), and start using them! Go to farmers' markets, co-ops, join a CSA (Community Supported Agriculture), shop at Limbo, whatever--just eat your veggies!

Organic produce can cost more than non-organics, but we think buying organic is like health insurance: Avoiding cancer-causing chemicals will pay off.

Also, re-use your bags, and bring them to the market with you.

Another consideration: "Veganic" farming is something new for a lot of us, but certainly important. Was your organic onion grown with blood or bone meal? What about manure from a meat-producing farm? Although it may not always be possible to know, it is a good idea to try to find out. Many farms are "veganic," though, and only use vegetable-based natural fertilizers.

~Bulk foods and other items available in bulk -

Many vegan staples are available in bulk: flours, dried fruits, nuts, seeds, legumes, pastas, grains, coffee, teas, oils, vinegars, sweeteners, snacks, and just about everything else can be purchased in bulk. Some stores even carry things like falafel, soup, and veggie burger mixes; tofu; olives; vegan cream cheese; and sea veggies in bulk. The reasons to buy in bulk, as already stated, are big ones. Save money, drastically reduce the amount of packaging you consume, and eat a more healthful, whole-foods-centered diet...all by buying in bulk! Bulk items are found just about everywhere now, even in the big chain groceries, as demand has increased.

Another advantage to buying in bulk is that you can purchase exactly the amount you need. Buy twenty-five pounds of rice, or just a cup at a time. You can stretch your budget by buying small amounts of expensive products that are usually sold in large quantities.

Bulk ingredients can be stored in your cupboard in old jars or bottles. Stores that sell bulk products have scales so that you can measure the tare weight of your container (so you aren't paying for the weight of the container), and so you can weigh out exactly how much you want. Weigh your containers and write the tare weight on them before filling them. Also write the bin number and price per pound of the item you're buying. The cashier will weigh your items when you check out, then subtract the tare weight of the container.

~Canned and jarred food -

Be sure to plan for that pesky natural disaster by stocking your pantry with canned foods. You may also want to have them on hand for when a recipe calls for cannellini beans or diced tomatoes. We think it's a good idea to have a selection of canned items on hand, including things like coconut milk, olives, tomato products, a variety of beans, salsa, artichoke hearts, jams, chili, and soups. Trader Joe's and Grocery Outlet are great places to stock up on canned and jarred foods.

While we encourage people to use fresh fruits and vegetables, a well-stocked vegan kitchen will need to include canned goods, and so will your bomb shelter!

~In the fridge -

First, stock your fridge with a variety of fresh, organic produce. It's also nice to have staples like non-dairy milks, Vegenaise (vegan mayo), Earth Balance non-hydrogenated vegan margarine, tofu, tempeh, and seitan. Some people like to have various analogs like Tofurky slices; veggie dogs; vegan cheeses, sour cream and cream cheese, etc.; however, none of these is necessary, and can be considered occasional provisions. Some vegans might not want to live without a supply of coffee creamer and Gimme Lean veggie sausage, while others are fine without them.

~In the freezer -

Again, what one person feels is a staple, another can do without. Here are some frozen staples we like: juice and fruit for smoothies, spinach, peas, veggie blends, burgers, fries, pie crusts, ice cream, waffles, hash browns, snacks like spring rolls and dumplings, pies and pastries that can be baked when you want them, and home-prepared soups, burritos and other ready-to-eat meals. Other frozen products available include onion rings, breaded mushrooms, pizzas, burritos, and packaged meals. Tofu can be purchased in bulk and frozen, although freezing tofu changes its texture. Try for yourself and see if you like it. It is also a good idea to keep flours, cornmeal, oats, nuts and seeds in the freezer to keep them from going bad.

~On a budget -

Your best bet is to plan meals by using cookbooks, buy bulk, whole-foods ingredients, and make big batches that will last a few days. For example, cook a pot of beans using bulk dried beans and make a pan of brown rice. This is your canvas for three or more days. You can have beans and rice on the first day, burritos on the second day, and chili on the third. Or you can make eight or ten burritos and freeze most of them. With only a few additional ingredients, you've got three days' worth of meals. Also, as mentioned before, utilizing discount stores helps keep food costs low.

Another resource which can be accessed in times of financial strain is the amazing food pantry. There are places to obtain free food all over Portland. Food pantries usually allow clients to pick up one good-sized "food box" a month. Information about food pantries can be found by calling 211, social services info line, or www.211info.org. These pantries can provide almost all of one's food needs and are stocked with all sorts of vegan foods, most of which are unwanted by the typical pantry patron.

Vegan Business Owner Profile:
Chad Miller - Food Fight! Grocery

How long have you been vegan and what turned you on to it originally?

Emiko and I went vegan at the same time, October of 1997. It just seemed a natural progression from vegetarianism, which I had gotten into through punk rock back in 1991. Emiko had only gone vegetarian months before on her own before we met, Emiko had gone vegetarian on her own as a form of "cutting out the bad stuff from my life."

Why did you start Food Fight?

We were tired of going to multiple stores to find the things we wanted. One store might have everything we wanted except for good bread for example. The store with good bread didn't have friggin' Vegenaise. It kinda started out as a joke about a vegan convenience store and just took off.

As a hub for vegan food but also local activists, how would you like to see more vegans get involved in activism in Portland?

We would like people to get involved In ANY way possible. Anything along the "activism" spectrum, from writing letters, to outreach, to direct action. We feel strongly that veganism can't just be a consumer movement or trend and that people need to keep pushing their comfort levels on behalf of the animals. They have far too few people on their side and no time to waste.

What are your favorite things about being vegan in Portland?

Choices. Almost anywhere you go, there are vegan options. And people here are generally well informed about what that means. You rarely have to go into detail

What products do you carry that you never thought there would be vegan versions of?

Lots of things have changed since we opened. We now have vegan versions of Snickers, caviar, haggis, Cheez-Its. It's really pretty goofy, but great. Vegan cheese has come a long way too. Before too long, all those "I'd go vegan if only I didn't have to give up xxx...." excuses will all disappear.

Vegan Essentials in the Kitchen

Rice, Grains, Noodles, & Pasta:

Basmati and/or Jasmine Rice, Brown Rice, Couscous, Quinoa, Rice Noodles, Yakisoba Noodles, Spaghetti, Macaroni, Penne

Non-Perishable Goods (Cans & Jars):

Amy's Soups, Chickpeas, Black Beans, Kidney Beans, Coconut Milk, Pineapple Chunks, Tomato/Marinara Sauce, Tomato Paste, Whole Tomatoes, Sundried Tomatoes, Artichoke Hearts, Sliced Olives

Non-Perishable (Other Pantry Items):

Dave's Killer Bread, Tortillas, Nutritional Yeast, Nuts (e.g. almonds, cashews, peanuts, pecans, pistachios, walnuts, etc.), Dried Fruit (e.g. apples, banana chips, mango, pineapple, berries, etc.), Energy Bars (e.g. Clif, Luna, Larabar, Vega), Protein Powder (e.g. hemp, yellow pea, Vega, etc.), Greens Powder (e.g. VitaSea, Trader Joe's, etc.)

Perishable Goods:

Extra-Firm Tofu, Tempeh, Tempeh Bacon/Smart Bacon, Tofurkey Slices, Vegan Chick'n Strips, Smart Ground, Gimme Lean Sausage, Soyrizo, Vegan Soy or Rice Cheese (e.g. Teese, Follow Your Heart, ... etc.), Vegan Parmesan Cheese, Natural Peanut Butter, Jam or Preserves, Hummus, Salsa, Vegan Milk (e.g. Soy, Rice, Almond, or Hemp), Earth Balance Margarine, Miso

Fresh Fruits & Veggies:

Bananas, Apples, Oranges, Berries, Mixed Greens, Spinach, Kale, Tomato, Cucumber, Onions (Red, Yellow, Sweet, etc.), Bell Peppers (Green, Red, etc.), Asparagus, Broccoli, Avocado, and whatever else you like!

Frozen Foods:

Frozen Fruit (Blueberries, Strawberries, etc.), Edamame, Meatless Meatballs, Vegan Veggie Burgers (e.g. Amy's, Boca Burgers, etc.), Soy Nuggets

Oils, Vinegars & Condiments:

Extra-Virgin Olive Oil, Canola Oil, Peanut Oil, Coconut Oil, Flax Oil, Balsamic Vinegar, Apple Cider Vinegar, Red Wine Vinegar, Vegenaise, Ketchup, Dijon Mustard, Bragg Liquid Aminos, Soy Sauce, Sweet & Sour Sauce, Hot Sauce (e.g. tobasco, Aardvark sauce, etc.), Pure Maple Syrup, Agave Nectar

Herbs and Seasonings:

Black Pepper, Sea Salt, Seasoned Salt, Basil, Cayenne, Cinnamon, Cloves, Cumin, Garlic Powder, Ginger, Italian Seasoning, Nutmeg, Oregano, Paprika, Rosemary, Thyme, Tumeric

For Baking:

All-Purpose Flour, Whole-Wheat Flour, Gluten Flour, Chickpea Flour, Baking Soda, Baking Powder, Organic Cane Sugar, Cornstarch, Pure Vanilla Extra, Raisins, Vegan Semi-Sweet Chocolate Chips, Cocoa Powder, Rolled Oats, Shredded Coconut, Flax Seeds, Ener-G Egg Replacer

Vegan Fitness
An Interview with Ed Bauer and Robert Cheeke

Name: Ed Bauer
Titles: 24 Hour Fitness Certified Personal Trainer, National Exercise & Sports Trainers Association Certified Personal Fitness Trainer

Name: Robert Cheeke
Titles: President of Vegan Bodybuilding & Fitness, Director/ Producer of *Vegan Fitness Built Naturally* and *Vegan Brothers in Iron*, National Event Coordinator for VEGA, World's Most Recognized Vegan Bodybuilder, 2-time Natural bodybuilding Champion, Author of *Vegan Bodybuilding & Fitness – The Complete Guide to Building Your Body On A Plant-Based Diet* (due out 9/09)

How long have you been vegan?

Ed Bauer: I have been vegan since March of 1996. I was 16 years old.

Robert Cheeke: Growing up in Oregon, I lived on a farm and had many farm animals as pets. I always had a love and appreciation for animals and from an early age, I was concerned about their well-being. However, it wasn't until Dec. 8, 1995 that I decided to give up consuming meat for good. My older sister, Tanya, was organizing an Animal Rights Week at my high school. I decided out of respect for her (a vegan since the age of 15) that I would become a vegetarian for the week. I attended lectures, listened to speakers, read literature about animal cruelty and watched videos about factory farms and animal testing, and that week of becoming vegetarian, turned to a vegan lifestyle shortly after and has continued over the past 14 years. I don't see myself going back to a non-vegan diet at any point in my life. I feel my role as a vegan in the public eye is important because I can show many different sides of veganism, including a health and fitness aspect that many people may not be familiar with.

What inspired you originally to become vegan?

Robert Cheeke: My older sister Tanya was my inspiration for becoming vegan nearly 15 years ago. We're both still vegan today and in fact we keep in touch regularly and see each other in person weekly.   She's a very good friend of mine, one of my biggest supporters and continues to inspire me today.

I think I likely would have found the vegan lifestyle at some point in my life, but there is no telling when that would have been. The fact that veganism came into my life when I was a teenager allowed me to save so many more lives than if I had adopted a vegan lifestyle later on in life. It is never too late to become vegan and nobody is better than anyone else based on how long they have lived a vegan lifestyle, but I am just grateful and thankful that it came into my life when it did because it changed my life forever.   I'm known as the world's most recognized vegan bodybuilder and have been for ten years. That wouldn't have been possible without my sister's influence fifteen years ago. My jobs, my interests, and my group of friends are all based around my lifestyle.

Ed Bauer: What originally inspired me to become vegan was at that time in my life, I was ready to start being honest with myself. I knew where meat and dairy came from, but I didn't know from what method or if the reason was justified. Plus I always knew that it is not all right to kill, and up until that time, I did a pretty good job convincing myself that my hands were clean. With the help of some friends and music from hardcore bands like Earth Crisis, I reconsidered my dietary and lifestyle choices. I then read John Robbins' *Diet for a New America* and I could no longer justify any other choice except veganism. The inhumane conditions that animals are kept in, the treatment of animals as if they were machines, the hormones and antibiotics that they are force-fed, the vicious and brutal murder of these sentient creatures, all of this was just too much. I cannot be a person who truly believes in peace, health, and happiness while supporting such a barbaric ritual that tortures, enslaves and murders innocent creatures. To truly have peace in your life, the answer is veganism. There simply is no other way.

Does a vegan diet automatically mean a healthier diet?

Ed Bauer: A vegan diet does not automatically mean healthier. A vegan diet simply means you remove all products that come from an animal: beef, chicken, fish, pork, all flesh foods, dairy and eggs. A healthy diet includes fewer refined processed food, more fruits, vegetables, nuts, seeds, legumes, whole grains, and water. Whole, plant-based foods are filled with a wide variety of vitamins and minerals and are high in fiber, while animal products have fewer nutrients, more saturated fats, cholesterol and too much hard-to-digest protein. If you truly want to consume a healthy diet, a vegan diet rich in whole foods; a variety of legumes, nuts and seeds; and a multivitamin will be your best bet. Your chances of getting diagnosed with heart disease, various cancers, and osteoporosis will be greatly reduced. Remember that people may say that animal products have certain things that you cannot get in a plant-based diet. Think about that for a second. Where do you think that animal gets those nutrients? I think it will lead back to the plants that the animal consumes. It is only logical.

Robert Cheeke: One of my favorite quotes is from Professional Vegan Triathlete Brendan Brazier, who said, "Just because it's vegan, it doesn't mean it's good for you."

Vegan doesn't automatically mean healthier. There are plenty of junk food vegan diets that are nutritionally inferior to the non-vegan diet of someone who eats mostly plants and only animal products occasionally. The argument for health will always be a challenging one, whether vegans (including myself) want to hear or admit that or not. We do have a superior moral and ethical argument for veganism. That goes without question and is supported by some of the brightest people on the planet. But when it comes to discussing health specifically, there are lots of opinions, lots of ideas, and many different feelings and theories as to which diet is "best."

I believe that a full plant-based diet is one of the best nutrition programs someone could follow. It's hard to say concretely that a 100% plant-based diet is "healthier" than a 99% plant-based diet with occasional consumption of meat. In fact, you can't really make that argument from a health or nutrition standpoint but you can from a moral standpoint every time. What is important to recognize is that some of the worst foods to eat for health are foods that vegans and non-vegans alike can consume. They are in fact, high refined-sugar foods and heavily processed foods like common snacks; potato or corn chips, bread products, candies, etc. There are countless foods that are very bad for our health that do not contain any animal products. What we really need to focus on is going back to the basics and start consuming more whole foods. Whole foods are foods that are grown in a garden or in the ground, or on a bush or on a tree in their natural state, such as fruits, vegetables, nuts, grains and seeds. When we consume more plant-based whole foods and reduce our consumption of processed and refined foods, we become healthier. In addition to the processed and refined-sugar foods, animal products such as dairy have profound adverse effects on our health as well. Cholesterol consumption is related to problems with blood flow, artery constriction, and eventually heart and overall health problems. Dairy intake is connected with all kinds of health issues from allergies, to the reduction of bone density, to lack of calcium in the body (dairy is not a good source of calcium as is commonly believed), and a long list of other health problems that make dairy even worse than many meats when it comes to overall health.

All that being said, it is very hard to say that a vegan diet is always healthier than a non-vegan diet because there are countless examples of where that is not the case (as in the examples of the vegan junk food diets packed full of vegan processed foods, snacks, treats and sweets that many consume every day). Our primary objective should be a real, sincere, and honest attempt to incorporate more plant-based whole foods into our diets and naturally we will reduce our consumption of unhealthy foods including animal products, heavily processed foods and refined sugars. It is also imperative that we take a real hard look at the moral and ethical dilemma we're faced with every time we cause pain or suffering to non-human animals, including every meal we eat that has animal products in it.

Robert, what has competing taught you about health?

Robert Cheeke: Bodybuilding taught me about consuming the healthiest foods, consuming a wide variety of foods, consuming helpful supplements, levels of discipline which most people never get to experience in their lives. Bodybuilding has also taught me that it's not the perfect way to live. We restrict our carbohydrate intake, our sodium intake, our water intake and manipulate our bodies and our overall health in other deliberate ways in order to achieve a certain look, at least for a short period of time, even if we know it is unhealthy practice.

As a competitive bodybuilder I've also learned that you can't just "listen to your body" as some preach, because there are many things that you'll never feel, such as your kidneys or liver suffering or struggling to process high amounts of protein. You can't simply rely on listening to your body. Your body doesn't always tell you when your lower back has had just about enough and then finally gives in leaving you unable to walk for a period of time, which happened to me earlier this year. Rather than listening to your body you can listen to reason and observe sensible behavior and predict outcomes based on rationale. Bodybuilding can be one of the healthiest ways to live if you extract the healthiest principles and discard those which can be counter productive to health or have adverse side effects to wellness. Bodybuilding has taught me to be more aware and more observant of everything around me. That is a natural by-product of living a 24-hour a day, 365 days a year sport that is influenced and impacted by literally every decision we make from sleep, to food, to exercise.

Ed, what do you focus on with your vegan clients?

Ed Bauer: I focus on the same things as I do with my non-vegan clients. Properly timed, properly planned meals of a combination of protein, carbs and healthy fats, resistance training for maintaining or gaining muscle mass; overall caloric deficit or surplus depending on client goals; cardiovascular programming for heart health, speed, endurance, or assistance with a caloric deficit; focus on the short-term goal instead of the long-term; and a positive outlook to ensure results.

As weight lifters, is a lack of protein a problem?

Robert Cheeke: As a weight lifter and competitive bodybuilder protein is one of the most crucial and essential components of nutrition to pay attention to. It is amusing when vegans come up to me and say, "Ha! I knew we didn't need to eat lots of protein to be fit," when they observe me wearing a Vegan Bodybuilding t-shirt. I inform them that actually, I eat hundreds of grams of protein a day, far more than is advised to the general public and far more than almost anyone I know aside from other bodybuilders. To these people who believe that I'm not eating protein because I'm vegan, I'm quick to explain that although I'm not eating *animal* protein, I do in fact eat quite a bit of protein to build and maintain my physique as a bodybuilder.

If we are exerting ourselves with effort and intensity and if we are using resistance training or weight lifting, it becomes imperative that we consume adequate amounts of protein, roughly 1 gram of protein per pound of body weight. This is far more than the average person needs, but as weight training athletes, we have above-average nutritional needs. Protein intake becomes excruciatingly important in a bodybuilding and weight training lifestyle. Without adequate consumption of protein we cannot improve, repair, rebuild, or support muscle fibers broken down from weight training. However, excess protein consumption above 1 gram of protein per pound of body weight can cause creatinine levels in the body to rise and tax the kidneys, which process all protein just as the liver processes alcohol. Since too much protein is tough on our kidneys, we have to find that delicate balance of about 1 gram of protein per pound of body weight and thrive. If you have questions about your protein intake, get some blood work done and it will reveal what you need to work on, raising or lowering your protein intake to maintain a healthy homeostasis within the body.

Ed Bauer: As a vegan weight lifter, protein is definitely not a problem. Weight lifters need more protein than the average adult, but not as much as most "fitness" articles would say. Protein is in most everything. A few high protein vegan options are tofu, tempeh, seitan, black beans, peas, almonds, kidney beans, pumpkin seeds, hummus, quinoa, hemp seeds, peanut butter, sprouted breads, veggie meat substitutes, whole grains and vegan protein powders such as soy, rice, pea, or hemp. A veggie salad with pumpkin seeds and one piece of sprouted bread has about 20 grams of protein. A smoothie with orange juice, berries, a banana, some ground flax seed, kale, and a tablespoon of brown rice protein has about 30 to 32 grams of protein. A veggie sandwich on sprouted whole grain bread has about 15 grams of protein. Add hummus and that will be around 20 grams. A bean and rice burrito from one of Portland's fine vegan-friendly establishments has about 20 to 25 grams of protein. These are all ideal protein servings for a single meal. Plus, with the varied sources of protein, you can be assured they are complete proteins.

What is a good program for losing weight?

Robert Cheeke: In order to lose weight we need to understand what our caloric intake requirements are based on our age, gender, height, weight and activity level, and then create a nutrition fat-burning program coupled with an exercise program that supports it.

In general, the best way to lose weight is to burn more calories than we're consuming and to do consistent exercise every day while eating healthy plant-based whole foods. It's really not that difficult.

Keeping stress levels low, getting adequate sleep and finding meaning in what we're doing are all great ways to support our efforts to lose weight. Being accountable and really doing what we say we're doing and what we think we're doing will help get us there more rapidly, which improves our mood, gives us encouragement and propels our drive to continue to improve. Keep cortisol (stress hormone) levels low, keep your adrenal glands functioning optimally, and really put in an honest effort to keep yourself dedicated to exercise and nutrition in order to achieve your goals of weight loss.

Ed Bauer: That is an easy one. If you want to lose *weight*, eat less and move more.

If you want to lose *fat*, eat less, watch your protein and fiber levels, and resistance train. That means lift weights. Muscle not only makes you look and feel better, it keeps your metabolism up all day every day. That equals more calories burned and more fat burned. So if you want to lose weight the right way, make it fat weight that you lose and lift weights. I'm talking to you!

What is a good program for a vegan to add strength?

Ed Bauer: Include a full-body structural exercise for most workout sessions, such as squats, dead lifts, overhead press, etc. Besides that, perform 2 to 3 exercises per body part one to two times a week, with three to five sets of three to six reps each with heavy weight, with a few minutes' rest in between. Only use this training protocol for six to eight weeks, then change the routine to provide your body with a new adaptation phase. Get lots of rest in between workout sessions and enjoy eating the right foods to recover and come back stronger.

Robert Cheeke: The best way to add strength is to lift heavy weights and eat lots of food. It doesn't matter whether someone is vegan or not. For anyone to add strength they need to test their muscles more than they have before. Increased levels of stress on the body cause the muscles, tendons, ligaments, and bones to respond by getting stronger. When this is supported by a sound nutrition program that incorporates adequate and sufficient quantities of protein and overall calories, strength is increased and often muscle size follows.

Most athletes' preferred method of training for strength is to lift heavy weights for few repetitions. It is also important to choose compound (multi-joint) mass-building exercises such as squats, deadlifts, and bench presses. When you use basic compound exercises and use free weights for low reps and heavy weight you are sure to put on some size and some strength, and getting stronger is one of the most fun and most addicting aspects of exercising in the first place. Focus on training each muscle group hard once or twice a week and cover the entire body, giving it necessary time to rest before that same muscle group is trained again. Exercise with intent and intensity and results will follow.

What are the benefits of having a workout partner or a trainer?

Ed Bauer: Some of the benefits of having a workout partner are their ability to keep you motivated, their ability to keep you accountable by setting the appointment, and their presence as a spot for some of the more difficult exercises. The benefits of working with a trainer are all of those a workout partner can provide, plus the ability to ensure that the most effective and efficient workouts are being performed. The client's goals can be achieved through proper nutrition and supplementation recommendations, stretching and flexibility, cardiovascular training, resistance exercise selection, and professional assistance to put this all together.

Robert Cheeke: Having a workout partner or trainer can make all the difference. My greatest experiences lifting weights have been with personal trainers and training partners. It adds elements of fun, competitiveness, and education. It makes training something to look forward to if you don't have the intrinsic motivation to get to the gym with enthusiasm on your own. It provides an atmosphere for support, ensures you have someone to spot you and it creates some sort of mutual accountability as you rely on each other to be there each and every session whereas if you always trained on your own you could easily skip a day.

If you don't have a training partner, find someone at the gym that looks like they are capable of spotting you when you need help with an exercise. You can also observe who is training at the same time as you on a regular basis and offer to give them a spot or ask them for a spot and before you know it you could have a new training partner.

Some people overlook personal trainers as something unnecessary but they can be of invaluable help if you're open to learning and reaching your full potential. Your personal trainer doesn't have to be vegan. All exercises are the same whether you're vegan or not, and not all trainers know a lot about nutrition anyway. Some do, but by and large I'm a much bigger fan of finding a personal trainer who really enjoys what they are doing, focuses their undivided attention on their clients, has a positive attitude, and is friendly and motivating. I enjoy surrounding myself with people who bring out the best in me and that is the advice I would give to those looking for their own personal trainer or training partner.

What should you eat after a workout?

Robert Cheeke: Post-workout nutrition is a big part of my whole bodybuilding life and should be a big part of any athlete's life. A combination of protein, fats and carbohydrates should be consumed immediately post-workout. Protein is the most pressing need because it helps repair, build, and grow muscle fibers damaged during exercise. I like to consume protein drinks after a workout because liquid nutrition is so easy to absorb and it's simply easier to consume lots of nutrition through liquid sources than to chew lots of dense foods. I like to use products such as Vega, a plant-based, whole food, all-in-one powder that has protein, but also vitamins, minerals, essential fats, digestive enzymes and more. Vega is vegan and free of common allergens. I also enjoy taking the amino acid L-Glutamine, which is the most important amino acid for muscle recovery and growth. It also plays a very tangible role in recovery from exercise so we can go back and train hard with muscles that have been properly nourished.

In general, athletes should look to replenish glycogen used up during exercise and vitamins and minerals lost during exercise by eating a variety of foods and taking in a nutrition shake based on hemp, pea, rice or some other plant-based protein, ensuring the consumption of proteins, fats and carbohydrates in the post-workout nutritional window of opportunity within about an hour after exercise.

Ed Bauer: The best thing to consume after a workout is around 20-35 grams of easy-to-digest protein as well as 30–60 grams of simple carbohydrate. These numbers vary depending on the size and goals of the individual. I, for example, weigh around 172 pounds and use around 30 grams of protein from non-gmo brown rice protein and non-gmo pea protein isolate along with a banana and/or juice to provide about 50 grams of simple carbohydrate. The protein is needed to repair the muscle tissue that was damaged during the workout. The simple carbohydrates are needed to spike the insulin levels which will assist in proper protein and amino acid utilization, as well as to restore the blood glycogen levels that were lowered during energy production. If one were to consume only protein after an intense workout, the protein would convert to carbohydrate to restore the lowered blood glycogen levels and never get to muscle repair, which is the reason we consume protein in the first place. Therefore, one would not get stronger or leaner because protein was unable to serve its intended function. Carbohydrate alone cannot repair muscle tissue either, as carbohydrate can not convert to protein. The take home message is consume protein and simple carbs within one hour after a workout for recovery and proper progression.

Why is form important?

Ed Bauer: Proper form is needed to help prevent possible injury. It is highly advised to lift a weight that one can lift with good form, with proper muscle activation at a controlled speed.

Robert Cheeke: Form and technique are extremely important because they help prevent injury and ensure the proper muscles are being trained in the way they are designed to be trained in a given exercise. I have injured myself a number of times in the past because I have not paid enough attention to proper form. One of the best ways to learn good form for weight lifting exercise is to learn from an experienced personal trainer or an experienced weight lifter or bodybuilder. Using good form can help prolong your lifting career and allow you to achieve greater gains than you would with poor form. Many people, including professional bodybuilders, lift with poor technique, relying on momentum and gravity to move weight around rather than engaging the muscles that they are attempting to train. However, you are sure to have your best results when you learn proper technique and stick to it.

Why should vegans focus on bodybuilding and fitness?

Robert Cheeke: The greatest impact we can have on anyone is directly a result of leading by positive example. This is evident when we consider any role models that we have for ourselves. We look up to others because they inspire us in some way and because they lead by example in areas of interest that resonate with us. We aspire to be like those who inspire us. When vegans go against the stereotype of being weak and scrawny and give a new perspective for what is possible on a plant-based vegan diet, it inspires other vegans to get stronger, and is encouraging for non-vegans who previously feared a plant-based lifestyle because of the common physical stereotypes attached to it.

I have dedicated my life to the Vegan Bodybuilding & Fitness lifestyle and I think it is immensely important for us to show this side of veganism. I started my own company Vegan Bodybuilding & Fitness around this idea back in 2002 and have since been promoting it heavily changing the way we think about food.

Ed Bauer: Vegans shouldn't necessarily focus on bodybuilding. There are a lot of us out there that do, but what is more important is to focus on fitness. Fitness is defined as good health or physical condition, especially as the result of exercise and proper nutrition. There are many reasons out there to adopt a vegan lifestyle, from reducing your carbon footprint, to reducing your risk of various health conditions, to spiritual or religious concerns, to the ethical treatment of animals, but regardless of what reason brought you to veganism in theory or in practice, everyone can benefit from being physically fit. From increased energy, improved cardiovascular endurance, lower body fat mass, greater strength, improved self image, greater lean muscle tissue, and enhanced feelings of well being, the benefits of fitness are easily worth the time and effort.

Thank you for taking the time to read this and I wish you the best in health and happiness.

Vegan Food Pyramid

Sometimes it's hard to know how much you need to eat of any one particular food.

Joshua Wold has put together a comprehensive vegan food pyramid to help give his fellow vegans a better idea what portions of foods they should eat. It's modeled after the USDA food pyramid. He has posters and desktop backgrounds available on his website: www.veganfoodpyramid.com.

He's been kind enough to allow us to use his pyramid as an example of a healthy vegan diet in our guidebook.

Thanks Joshua!

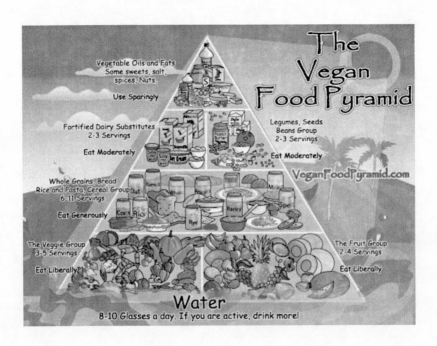

Common Animal Ingredients List

As vegans, most of us know the basics: no meat, no milk, no eggs, and no cheese. However, there are a lot of food additives that we don't often think about, but which are in most things we eat from day to day. Most people realize that we also don't eat honey, or use ingredients with beeswax, but almost no one thinks of gelatin as an animal ingredient, because not everyone realizes where it comes from.

Listed below are a list of common animal ingredients you find in everyday items, as well as a brief description of what they are and where they are often found. This is not a definitive list, only a guide.

Albumen (or Albumin): Another name for egg whites, this is used as a coagulating agent. Often found in products like baked goods and some candies, but can also be used in some wines.

Allantoin (also Alcloxa and Aldioxa): Usually derived from uric acid in mammals. Often found in cosmetics and anti-bacterial cleansers.

Alpha-Hydroxy (also Alpha-Hydroxi) Acids: One commonly used alpha-hydroxy acid (lactic acid) may be derived from milk. Used in cosmetics, primarily anti-aging creams, as well as some shampoos.

Ambergris: Found in sperm whale intestines. Sometimes used in perfumes, as well as flavoring in foods & beverages.

Angora: Bunny fur. Used in clothing.

Biotin (also Vitamin H or Vitamin B Factor): Derived from milk. Often found in cosmetics and shampoos.

Carmine (also Cochineal or Carmic Acid): Crushed beetle shells. (Seriously!) Used as a red coloring agent in everything from food and drink to cosmetics.

Casein (also Caseinate or Sodium Caseinate): Milk protein. Found in foods and cosmetics. Be careful of soy cheeses, as they may contain milk proteins (not all soy cheese is vegan).

Cashmere: Goat fur. Used in clothing.

Castoreum: A product derived from the genitals of muskrats & beavers. Used in perfumes and incense.

Catgut: Animal intestines. Used in surgical sutures, but also to string tennis rackets and musical instruments.

Cholesterol: A steroid alcohol derived from animal fat, tissue and blood.

Civet: Musk obtained from the genital region of a cat-like mammal. Used in perfumes.

Collagen: Derived from animal tissue. Used in skin creams.

Cortisone: A steroid hormone derived from pig adrenal glands. Used as a drug to treat a variety of ailments.

Diglycerides (also Monoglycerides and Glycerin): A byproduct of soap manufacture and usually derived from animal fat. Used in foods, cosmetics, soaps, medicines, toothpastes, gum and plastics.

Elastin: Protein found in cow tendons. Used in hair and skin products.

Estrogen: Found in female horse urine. Primarily found in birth control pills.

Gelatin: Obtained by boiling animal parts (usually bones, skin and ligaments) with water. Is used in food products and cosmetics. Also used in photographic film and as a coating for some pills and vitamins.

Honey: Produced by bees as food for bees. Used in foods and cosmetics.

Keratin: Protein obtained from ground hooves, horns, quills and hair of various animals. Used in hair care products.

Lactose: A sugar found in mammal milk. Used in food products and cosmetics.

Lanolin: Found in sheep oil glands. Used in cosmetics, lotions and lip balms.

Pepsin: A clotting agent found in pig stomachs. Used in cheese production.

Propolis: Produced by bees. Used in personal care products, including some toothpastes.

Rennet: A coagulant found in cow stomachs. Used in cheese production and for other coagulated dairy foods, like yogurt and custard.

Royal Jelly: Secretion from the throat glands of honey bees. Used in cosmetics.

Silk: Produced by silkworms to make cocoons. Used for clothing and in cosmetics.

Stearic Acid: Derived from tallow. Used in a variety of foods, cosmetics and personal care products.

Tallow: Rendered animal fat. Used in a variety of food products, cosmetics and personal care products. Also used in crayons, paints, wax paper, rubber and lubricants.

Vitamin D-3: Obtained from a variety of sources, including fish liver oil and egg yolks. Used in vitamin supplements and personal care products.

Whey: Milk protein. Found in a variety of foods, as well as protein supplements.

Veganize It!

These days, being vegan couldn't be easier! Although that is true all over the country, it is especially true here in Portland. We have a vegan restaurant to satisfy almost any craving and new choices are being added every year. That said, you don't have to live in Portland--or any other extremely vegan-friendly city--to enjoy your old childhood favorites. Anyone who has access to a health food store like Whole Foods, a locally-run co-op, or even one of the many mainstream grocery stores with a natural-foods section can make amazing vegan alternatives to their favorite foods right at home. From vegan "chicken" strips to vegan mayo, there is a vegan alternative to virtually every food out there. This section outlines a few favorite menu items from childhood, then provides the vegan ingredients that can be used to make them.

For example, it's easy to veganize breakfast favorites like McDonald's-style sausage and egg McMuffins, pancakes, and scrambled eggs. Lunches can still include things like BLT sandwiches, egg salad sandwiches, and beef tacos. At dinner, the possibilities are endless, but lasagna, pizza, spaghetti and meatballs, and burgers are just a few dishes that can still be enjoyed by vegans. Below are a few different ideas for each meal and a list of vegan ingredients that can be used to make them.

Breakfast:

Sausage Egg Muffin Sandwich with Cheese

You can pick up vegan English muffins at any Whole Foods or Trader Joe's. You will also need some Tofutti brand vegan cheese slices, Gimme Lean vegan sausage, and some extra firm tofu. The secret ingredient, a little bit of Vegenaise brand vegan mayonnaise, adds a really great flavor and makes the sandwich taste just right.

Pancakes

It's easy to find a myriad of vegan pancake recipes in cookbooks and on websites. A favorite non-vegan recipe can also be adapted easily. All you need to do is replace the milk with your favorite non-dairy alternative, like Vanilla Almond Breeze brand almond milk. Substitute Ener-G brand egg replacer if the recipe calls for eggs. Using these simple alternatives, you can enjoy your favorite pancake recipe from when you were a kid, vegan style!

Scrambled Eggs

Making your favorite scrambled egg recipe vegan is easy! For a veggie scramble, just replace the eggs with crumbled tofu and you're all set. The trick to getting the tofu just right involves two ingredients: turmeric to give it a yellow color, and a little poultry seasoning (found in the spice section of any grocery store or market). If you like cheese on your scramble, just pick up some Follow Your Heart Vegan Gourmet cheese, available at most health food stores. The Monterey Jack flavor is great for scrambles. If you prefer a meatier flavor in your scramble, you can also throw in some Gimme Lean vegan sausage or Soyrizo vegan chorizo.

Lunch:

Bacon, Lettuce, and Tomato Sandwich (BLT)

BLT's are many people's favorite sandwich, and one of the easiest to veganize. Vegan sandwich bread is easy to find in any grocery store. Try Dave's Killer Bread, made locally right here in Portland. The rest of the ingredients are relatively simple: lettuce, tomato, mayo, and bacon. The mayo can be replaced with Vegenaise. Two possibilities to replace the bacon are LightLife brand Fakin' Bacon, made of tempeh; or LightLife brand Smart Bacon, made of soy and wheat gluten. Both are vegan and very tasty bacon alternatives. In general, Fakin' Bacon works well in salads as it adds a great flavor and a little protein at the same time. For BLT's, however, Smart Bacon wins because it gets nice and crispy when cooked in a frying pan with a little oil, and on a sandwich it tastes just like bacon!

"Egg" Salad

Tofu is not only a great replacement for eggs in scramble, but also works well as a replacement for eggs in "egg" salad. You can use all the usual ingredients for egg salad, except substitute tofu for the eggs and Vegenaise for the mayo.

"Beef" Tacos

"Beef" Tacos? Yes, you read that right! You can even make a vegan alternative to ground beef tacos. There are a number of different brands that make a fake ground meat from soy. In tacos, Yves brand Meatless Ground Taco Stuffers or LightLife brand Smart Ground Taco/Burrito style work best. The taco-flavored versions end up with a better taste overall than the original versions, although you still might want to add spice when cooking. If you like grated cheese in your tacos, you have few choices for that as well, including Teese brand cheddar flavor or Follow Your Heart Vegan Gourmet in either nacho or Monterey jack varieties.

Dinner:

Lasagne and Pizza

Both of these favorites can be made with either Teese Vegan Cheese or Follow Your Heart Vegan Gourmet. Both brands of vegan cheese come in a mozzarella variety and both taste great on pizza. The question of which one tastes the best is the subject of heated debates among the vegan community, so experiment for yourself and decide which side of the issue you come down on.

Spaghetti and Meatballs

Although some people do not realize it, most pasta is actually vegan by default. While some varieties contain egg or dairy, most are animal-free. As for the sauce, many great varieties at the regular grocery store are "accidentally vegan." Several varieties of vegan meatballs have also become pretty easy to find. Look for Nate's brand, or Trader Joe's generic brand of meatless meatballs. These are a great alternative to their non-vegan counterparts. They're so good that omnivores have even been tricked into believing that they are the real thing! There are also several great vegan alternatives to parmesan cheese, including Galaxy Nutritional Foods Vegan Parmesan Topping, and Parma Vegan Parmesan. Nutritional yeast can also be used as a parmesan replacement, although it gives foods a bit of a nutty flavor.

Burgers

Veggie burgers have existed for a very long time now and have become commonplace in most grocery stores across the country. Some brands and varieties, like Gardenburger brand Flame Grilled burgers and Morningstar Farms's Vegan Grillers, work well as a direct "meat replacement." Others, like Gardenburger's Black Bean Chipotle burger, don't taste or look meaty, but have a great alternative flavor. Adding a slice of Tofutti's American-style vegan cheese will turn any veggie burger into a cheeseburger.

Be careful: Not all veggie burgers are vegan! For example, Gardenburger's original variety, still found in many restaurants, contains eggs, milk, and cheese. If a particular product isn't clearly labeled vegan on the box, make sure to check the ingredients.

Dairy- and Egg-Free Baking

Dairy Replacers

Milk Alternative: Any replacement milk can be used. This includes "milk" made from soy, rice, oat, almond, and even hemp. Soymilk works the best as a replacement.

Butter Alternative: It is best to use a non-hydrogenated margarine or shortening made from palm oil. Coconut oil can also be used as a butter replacement. A regular oil may not work in a particular recipe.

Buttermilk Alternative: Simply add 1 tsp. lemon juice or cider vinegar per one cup of milk replacement. Stir, and let stand a few minutes.

Milk Powder Alternative: A non-dairy milk equivalent in a powdered form should be used. A liquid replacement will not work. Two brands which work well in baking include "Better than Milk" Soy Powder and DariFree Milk Powder Alternative made from potato. If a recipe calls for less than 2 Tbsp of the milk powder, you can simply omit the ingredient with good results.

Egg Replacers

Flaxseeds: Use 1 part seed to 4 parts water. Simmer 5-7 minutes. Allow "gloop" to cool, then pour into bowl lined with cheesecloth. Gather up the edges of the cloth and gently squeeze out the "gloop", until the cloth contains only seeds. 1 egg = 1/4 cup "gloop". *Uses: Contains distinctive flavor but great for texture. Works best for any baked good with a nutty or grainy taste.*

Flaxseed Meal: Mix together flaxseed meal and water, let sit a couple of minutes, then add as you would egg. 1 Tbsp flaxseed meal + 3 Tbsp water = 1 egg. *Uses: Contains distinctive flavor, but great for texture. Works best for any baked good with a nutty or grainy taste.*

Starches: Use like Ener-G Egg Replacer, which is a mixture of starches. Combine 1 Tbsp of starch (corn starch, potato starch, arrowroot starch) + 3 Tbsp water = 1 egg. *Uses: Since this is a simple egg replacer, works best with cookies. Eggs usually serve as a binder in recipes, and the starch mixture fills that role.*

Bananas: Use 1/4 - 1/3 cup of mashed banana per egg. *Uses: Great for muffins and quick breads that would benefit from a banana taste.*

Apple Sauce: Use 1/4 - 1/3 cup of applesauce per egg. *Uses: Works best in muffins and sweet breads. Leaves no additional taste.*

Blended Tofu: Silken tofu works best for this replacement. Blend before adding to recipe. 1/4 cup tofu = 1 egg. *Uses: great for cakes! Really moist and fluffy!*

Soy Yogurt: 1/4 cup soy yogurt = 1 egg. *Uses: great for quick breads and muffins.*

Brand Name Egg Replacers: Ener-G Egg Replacer, Bob's Red Mill Vegetarian Egg Replacer.

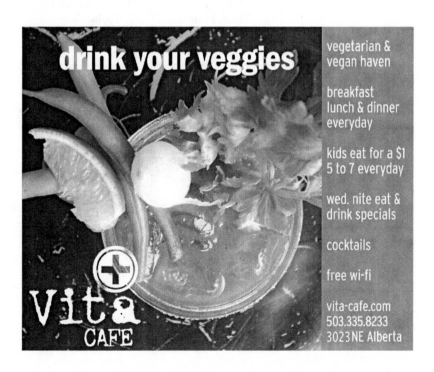

But What Can I Eat?
Meal Suggestions for the Week

	Monday	**Tuesday**
Breakfast	Veggie Sausage and **"Buttermilk Biscuits"** (page 52)	Tofu Scramble with Tempeh Bacon and Toast
Morning snack	Apple slices and peanut butter	Carrot Sticks w/ Tomato Basil Hummus
Lunch	Brown rice bowl with black beans, kale and soy ginger dressing	Tofurkey Sandwich with **Potato Salad** (page 47)
Afternoon Snack	Pita Chips with **Spinach-Lime Hummus** (page 53)	Fresh Herb Salad with Raspberry Vinaigrette
Dinner	**Shitake Mushroom Stroganoff** (page 40) with sautéed asparagus	Veggie Kebabs with **Sweet and Spicy Peanut Sauce** (page 46)
Dessert	**Summery Peanut Butter Chocolate Cups** (page 42)	Sweetpea Cookie

Wednesday	Thursday	Friday
Pancakes	**Raw Lemon Coconut Apple Bars** (page 49)	**Blueberry Muffins** (page 50)
Trail mix with dried fruit and nuts	Veggie sticks and Tofutti cream cheese	Fruit Smoothie
Quinoa Stuffed Collard Wraps (page 44)	BLT with "smart bacon" and soup	Pasta salad with whole-wheat pasta, veggies, beans, and oil and vinegar
Crackers with **Lima Bean "Cheese" Spread** (page 48)	Pita half with baba ghanouj	Primal Strip Jerky
Oven-roasted portobello steaks and **Tangy Asparagus** (page 51)	Pasta with Pesto and Sundried Tomatoes, steamed green beans	**Mac 'n Cheez** (page 54) with steamed broccoli
Coconut Cloud Cupcakes (page 45)	Temptations Cookie Dough ice cream	Voodoo Doughnut

Recipe Suggestions

All recipes provided courtesy of Try Vegan PDX members

Shitake Mushroom Stroganoff
by Heather Morgan

Ingredients:

3 TBSP Olive Oil
1 Large Onion, chopped
1/2 Green Bell Pepper, diced (optional)
2 cloves garlic, minced
1 lb shiitake mushrooms, sliced
1 1/2 Cup Vegetable broth
1 1/2 Cup Unsweetened hemp milk, or other high fat nut milk
3 TBSP all-purpose flour
1/3 Cup fresh parsley, chopped
2 TBSP Red wine vinegar
2 TBSP nutritional yeast
Salt, pepper and/or Spike to taste
Vegan sour creme (optional)

1 bag (8 oz) flat, vegan noodles

Instructions:

Bring 4 quarts water to a boil, salt lightly & add noodles. Cook approximately 8 minutes, or per package instructions. Drain.

While noodles are cooking, heat pan over medium heat and add oil. Add onion and garlic, sauteing until soft. Add mushrooms, increasing to medium-high heat and cook approximately 5 minutes, until mushrooms are limp & browned. Remove mushrooms and onions from heat and set aside in a bowl.

Add milk, broth, vinegar, and seasonings to skillet and heat over medium-high heat. Slowly add flour and nutritional yeast (to prevent clumping). Whisking often, bring mixture to a boil. Continue cooking until mixture has reduced and thickened to a good, saucy consistency.

Add sauce to noodles, and then stir in the mushrooms and onions. Top with vegan sour cream (optional) and garnish with parsley.

Makes 4 Servings

Vegan Musubi
by Deanna Cintas

Ingredients:

1 Package Nori sheets- make sure perforation is in 4" increments or so
1 Small bag of short grain white rice
Sliced vege ham loaf, marinated in Braggs Liquid Aminos

Instructions:

Cook rice in a saucepan or rice cooker according to package. I like to pour the rice into the rice cooker and add enough water to create ½" layer of water over the rice. While the rice is cooking, fry the sliced vege ham until slightly browned on each side. When rice is done lay out pieces of nori, making sure a small bowl of water is on hand to seal the seaweed together. Using a musubi mold is easiest, but if you do not have one, prepare to become a sculptor. Form ¼ c of rice on top of a nori sheet and in the middle. Add a piece of cooked vege ham and top with another ¼ c of rice. Fold seaweed over the rice and add some water to seal it. When the musubi are at room temperature they can be sliced in halves or plated as is.

Summery Peanut Butter Chocolate Cups
by Deanna Cintas

Ingredients:

2 bags vegan chocolate chips
1 Cup peanut butter
1 Cup powdered sugar (organic/ vegan)
2 Tbsp canola oil/ earth balance
1 Cup water/soy/hazelnut/almond milk

Instructions:

First get the portion sizes ready (mini cupcake tin, ice cube tray). Next prepare the peanut butter filling by mixing the peanut butter with ½ c of the powdered sugar, first with a spoon and then with your hands, until the consistency is pliable but not too firm, adding more powdered sugar if necessary. Break the peanut butter up into small teaspoon sized portions, making them either a coin shape (cupcake tin) or Tootsie roll shape (ice cube tray). Set them on a plate so they are ready to place once the chocolate is poured. Dribble a bit of the oil/ earth balance into each compartment and spread around compartment with finger. Melt one package of chocolate chips in a glass casserole dish in the microwave for 2 minutes. Stir to blend chocolate chips and add ½ c water/ milk to thin the consistency. Once chocolate is ready, spoon into individual compartments-distributing evenly. Add the peanut butter shapes, lightly placing on top of the chocolate. Melt the 2nd bag of chocolate in the microwave. Spoon out evenly on top of peanut butter until the peanut butter is covered. Place in freezer for at least an hour to set. Sprinkle half of the remaining powdered sugar on a plate. Run a knife along the perimeter of the compartment until the peanut butter cup is ready to give, carefully take out of compartment and place on plate. Once all cups are placed sprinkle the rest of the powdered sugar over the top to dust. Refrigerate until ready to serve.

Buffalo Tofu Sticks

by Chelsea Lincoln

Ingredients:

1 lb Tofu, firm
2 Tbsp Oil

Batter:

1/3 Cup Unbleached White Flour
2 tsp Paprika

Sauce:

1/4 Cup onion, chopped
2 cloves garlic, chopped
2 Tbsp tabasco chipolte hot sauce
2 Tbsp ketchup
1/4 tsp salt
1 Tbsp agave nectar
1 Tbsp lemon juice

Instructions:

Place all the sauce ingredients into a blender. Blend until the sauce has a smooth consistency and set aside. Cut the tofu block into 32 sticks. Mix together the flour and paprika for the batter in a wide mouthed bowl. Place the tofu sticks in the batter, a few at a time, to cover the tofu with the mixture. Set aside and finish covering all the tofu sticks with the batter.

Heat the oil in a large skillet on medium heat. You may need to cook these up in two batches. Place the battered tofu sticks in the skillet and cook until all sides are golden. Add the sauce and cook until all the sauce is absorbed and adhered to the tofu sticks.

Quinoa Stuffed Collard Wraps
by Chelsea Lincoln

Ingredients:

2 Cups cooked quinoa
1 Tbsp olive oil
1 yellow pepper, chopped
1 red repper, chopped
1 small onion, chopped
2 cloves garlic, minced
1 large tomato, chopped
1 Tbsp lemon juice
Salt and pepper to taste
8 collard green leaves, steamed

Instructions:

Look for pre-rinsed Quinoa or rinse the Quinoa before use. Prepare the quinoa as directed; set aside. Saute the onion, peppers and garlic in the oil until soft. Add the quinoa, tomato, lemon juice, salt and pepper. Cook for 5 minutes. Steam the collards and rinse them off with cold water so you can handle them. Dry the collards with a paper towel. Place the collard green leaf on a flat surface, with the smooth side down. Fill the lower, wider section of the leaf with the quinoa mixture, leaving room on the sides. Fold the leaf sides into the middle and roll the leaf up, similar to a burrito. Repeat with the rest of the collard green leaves.

Coconut Cloud Cupcakes

by Chelsea Lincoln

Vanilla Cake:

½ Cup soy margarine
1 ½ Cups organic raw sugar
½ Cup silken tofu
1 ½ Cups coconut milk
2 tsp vanilla
2 ½ Cups unbleached white flour
1 Tbsp baking powder
½ tsp salt

Coconut Frosting:

1/3 Cup margarine
2 Cups powdered sugar
½ Cup shredded coconut
2-5 Tbsp coconut milk

Instructions:

Cream together the margarine and sugar until smooth. Add the vanilla and blend, then the tofu and blend some more. Pour in the coconut milk and blend until incorporated. Add the flour, baking power and salt and blend until just mixed in. Fill greased muffin tins, or cupcake cups about 2/3 full with batter. Bake at 350 degrees for 20 minutes. When cupcakes are done, the top should spring back when lightly touched.

Frosting: Blend the powdered sugar and margarine together. Add coconut milk, a little at a time, until you reach the desired texture. Add in the shredded coconut. When frosting the cupcakes, dip the frosted top in more shredded coconut.

Makes 18 cupcakes.

Sweet and Spicy Peanut Sauce
by Deanna Cintas

Ingredients:

1 ½ Cup peanut butter
1 Tbsp Braggs Liquid Aminos
1 Tbsp Rooster Sauce (can sub for minced chilis, pepper flakes or cayenne- use 2 tsp instead)
1 Tbsp minced fresh ginger
¼ Cup pineapple juice
1 tsp apple cider vinegar
Hazelnut milk or coconut milk, to desired consistency
1 Tbsp minced garlic (optional)

Instructions:

Mix all together with a whisk. Add water or milk to thin as necessary. Use as a spread on kebabs before grilling and/ or as a dip after grilling.

Makes enough for 16 kebabs

Multi-Potato Salad Medley

by Deanna Cintas

Ingredients:

1 lb varied potatoes, cubed
A box soft tofu
¼ - 1/2 Cup Nayonnaise or Vegenaise
¼ Cup capers
1 Tbsp parsley
1 Tbsp Braggs Liquid Aminos
Kernels from one ear of corn
¼ Cup onion, diced
Squeeze of mustard
Shredded carrots (optional)
Sliced celery (optional)
Macaroni noodles (optional)
Salt and pepper to taste

Instructions:

Boil cubed potatoes for 5-8 minutes or until slightly tender. Strain and let cool. While the potatoes are boiling or cooling mix the rest of the ingredients together. When potatoes are cool enough add to blended mixture and stir well. Add more salt or Braggs to taste.

Lima Bean "Cheese" Spread

by Deanna Cintas

Ingredients:

1 can lima beans
1 head roasted garlic
½ lemon, juiced
1/2 Cup nutritional yeast
Salt to taste
A few drops of liquid smoke
A squeeze of mustard

Instructions:

Blend all together until a smooth consistency is reached. Feel free to add more nutritional yeast or salt to taste.

Raw Lemon Coconut Apple Bars

by Deanna Cintas

Ingredients:

1 Cup nuts (I used pecans, but macadamia nuts would be good too!)
1 ½ Cups dates
Juice of one lemon
1 Cup unsweetened coconut
2 ½ Cups apples

Instructions

Chop nuts. Use a bit of it to flour bottom of pan. Chop the rest of the ingredients and mix together with remaining chopped nuts. Press into baking pan. Chill for a few hours. Cut into 1" squares.

Makes 12 bars

Blueberry Muffins

by Chelsea Lincoln

Ingredients:

2/3 Cup unrefined cane sugar
2/3 Cup soy milk
2 Tbsp flaxseed meal + 6 Tb Water
1/3 Cup vegetable oil
1 tsp vanilla
2 Cups unbleached white flour
2 tsp baking powder
1/2 tsp salt
1 Cup fresh blueberries

Instructions:

Combine the flax and water and let sit a couple minutes. Mix together the sugar, soy milk, oil, vanilla and flax blend. Add the dry ingredients and stir until just combined. Fold in the blueberries, careful not to over mix. Fill greased muffin cups 3/4 full. Bake at 400 degrees for 20-25 minutes.

Makes 12 muffins

Tangy Roasted Asparagus

by Chelsea Lincoln

Ingredients:

24 asparagus stems
1 Tbsp olive oil
1 Tbsp lemon juice
2 cloves garlic, minced
1/4 tsp black pepper
1/4 tsp salt

Instructions:

Rinse off and chop off the ends of the asparagus. Spread the stems on a baking sheet. Combine the oil, lemon juice and minced garlic. Spread this on top of the asparagus and toss to cover all over the stems. I used my hands to do this. Sprinkle the salt and pepper on top and toss again to cover the stems well. Place this in the oven at 400 degrees and cook for 15-20 minutes, tossing the asparagus to cook evenly on the sheet.

Makes 4 servings

"Buttermilk" Biscuits

by Chelsea Lincoln

Ingredients:

4 Cups unbleached white flour
1 Tbsp baking powder
1 tsp baking soda
1 tsp salt
1 Tbsp sugar
1 Cup soy margarine
2 Cups soymilk + 1 Tbsp lemon juice

Instructions:

Combine the soymilk and lemon juice and let stand a few minutes. In a medium bowl, combine the flour, baking powder, baking soda, salt and sugar. Using a pastry cutter, cut the soy margarine into the flour mixture until pea sizes or smaller. Pour the soymilk mixture and blend until combined. Place dough on a floured work surface and knead a couple times. Spread the dough out to about 3/4 inch thickness and cut with a biscuit cutter. Place on a greased baking sheet and bake at 375°F for 15-18 minutes. Makes about 20 biscuits.

Spinach-Lime Hummus
by Deanna Cintas

Ingredients:

2 Cups cooked beans
½ Cup spinach
3 garlic cloves
¼ Cup balsamic vinegar
1 ½ limes, juiced
1 Tbsp salt, or to taste
½ Cup nutritional yeast.

Instructions:

Combine first 4 ingredients in blender or food processor. Add water until desired consistency is reached. Transfer mixture to a bowl and mix in last two ingredients. Serve with chips, or use as sandwich spread. Can also bake it at 325 for 10 minutes or so, to warm and use as a warm dip.

Vegan Mac 'n Cheez

by Heather Morgan

Ingredients:

16 oz. dry pasta of your choice

Cheez Sauce:

1 Cup raw cashews
1/3 Cup nutritional yeast
2 Cups water
1-2 Cloves fresh garlic, peeled
1/2 Tbsp salt
1 Tbsp arrowroot powder or corn starch
1 Tbsp lemon juice
Pepper to taste

Directions:

In a very dry blender, grind cashews until very fine and uniform consistency. Add water, garlic, salt, lemon juice and thickening agent of your choice (I prefer arrowroot powder, because it makes the sauce sort of stringy like cheese sauce, but corn starch works just as well) and puree for about a minute. Pour blender contents into a saucepan and cook over medium heat, stirring constantly, until sauce begins to boil. Allow sauce to boil for approximately 30 seconds, then remove from heat & whisk vigorously.

Cook pasta in accordance with the instructions and strain. Add cheez sauce and pepper to taste.

You will probably have a bit of sauce left over, I recommend using it as a dipping sauce for veggies (it goes great on broccoli).

Portland Vegan Profiles:
Peter Spendelow - NW Veg

How long have you been vegan and what turned you on to it originally?

I've been vegetarian since 1969 when I was still in high school because I couldn't stand the thought of animals being killed just for me to eat them. I didn't drop the dairy and cheese until about 8 years ago, after my son went vegan. I was amazingly ignorant back then about the factory farm conditions where eggs and milk are produced with virtually no regard to the animals involved and their interests.

What types of things does NW Veg do in the community?

We do 2 monthly potlucks with speakers, our annual VegFest, the Master Vegetarian Program, Veg 101 classes, a monthly dine-out, a book club, a monthly happy hour, a great newsletter, a veganic gardening group, a dining guide, and lots more that is aimed at supporting and educating people in moving to a plant-based diet.

How has veganism changed in Portland over the years?

When I first moved to Portland in 1985, I did not know of any vegetarian restaurants and only knew one or two that were particularly vegetarian-friendly. Now we list 7 vegan restaurants and 17 more vegetarian restaurants, plus a number of vegan and vegetarian food carts, in our dining guide.

What are your favorite places to eat out in Portland?

So many choices and I like lots of them. I really like hitting the all you can eat buffet at Vegetarian House for lunch on weekdays, though.

Tell us about Veg 101?

We have two sets of great classes. Veg 101 is a six-week series for people interested in or new to a plant-based diet, and pairs six one-hour cooking demonstrations with six one-hour classes. The Master Vegetarian Program is a nine-week program intended to provide solid background on all aspects of a plant-based diet, and similar to the Master Recycler and Master Gardener programs, class participants give back by providing volunteer service using the information they have gained in the class. For more information about both programs, visit www.nwveg.org.

Eating Out Late

Where do hungry vegans go at midnight when they're feeling peckish? Portland is notorious for having nothing open after 10pm. However, there are always options out there and some very good ones at that.

Aalto Lounge
3356 SE Belmont St
5 pm - 2 am, 7 days a week

Basement Pub
1028 SE 12th Ave
3 pm - 2 am, 7 days a week

Bye & Bye
1011 NE Alberta
4 pm - 2:30 am, M-F; 12 pm - 2:30 am Sat.-Sun.

Cactus Jack's
4342 SW Beaverton Hillsdale
9 am -12 am Sun; 11 am -12 am M; 11 am -2:30 am Tu - F; 9 am -
2:30 am Sat.

Dots
2521 SE Clinton St
12 pm - 2 am, 7 days a week

El Brasero (cart)
SE 12th & SE Hawthorne Cart Village
11 am - 9:30 pm, 7 days; might stay open later on Fridays and
Saturdays

Hammy's Pizza
2114 SE Clinton St
4 pm - 4 am, 7 days a week. Carry-out closes at 2:30 am.

Hungry Tiger Too
207 SE 12th
11 am - 2 am M-F; 9 am - 2 am Sat.; 9 am - 12 am Sun.

Langano Lounge
1435 SE Hawthorne Blvd
4 pm - 2 am, 7 days a week

LaurelThirst Public House
2958 NE Glisan St
11 am -1:30 am M-F (weeknight closing hours may vary); 9 am - 2 am Sat.-Sun.

Mash Tun
2204 NE Alberta St #101
4 pm - 12 am M-F; 12 pm - 12 am Sat.-Sun.

Pause
5101 N Interstate Ave
11:30 am - 1 am M-Sat.; 12 pm - 12 am Sun.

Perierra Creperie
SE 12th and Hawthone Cart Village
8 am - 3 am Tu-Sat; 9 am - 12 am Sun.

Potato Champion!
SE 12th and Hawthorne Cart Village
8 pm - 3 am W-Sat.

Report Lounge
1101 E Burnside St
4 pm - 2 am Tu - Sun.

Someday Lounge
125 NW 5th Ave
4 pm - 2 am M-W and Sat.; 6 pm - 2 am Th-F; 4 pm - 12 am Sun.

Tube Bar
18 NW 3rd Ave
5 pm - 2 am, 7 days a week

Vendetta
4306 N Williams Ave
3 pm - 1 am Sun-Th; 3 pm - 2am F-Sat

Voodoo Doughnut
22 SW 3rd Ave
Open 24 Hours a day, 7 days a week

Voodoo Too
1501 NE Davis
6am - 3am, 7 days a week

Whiffies Pie Cart
SE 12th and Hawthorne Cart Village
8 pm - 3 am, Tu-Sat

XV
15 SW 2nd Ave
4 pm - 2 am, 7 days a week

Portland Vegan Profiles:
Cindy Koczy - NW Veg

How long have you been vegan and what turned you on to it originally?

It will be going on 6 years in October '09. Initially I was interested in enjoying my health for years to come. I was sitting in the doctor's office and he wanted to prescribe 3 different medications! I had decided that was not for me, went home cleaned out my fridge and pantry and every day, with every meal, I'm sure I made the best decision. I love my life now.

How are you involved in the veg community?

I'm an active board member for a local non profit organization [NW Veg]. I go around and spread goodwill! I am part of the developing committee for The Master Veg Program, VegFest 2004-2009, potlucks, Veg 101 Program. I'm advocating for plant based diets daily.

How has veganism changed your life?

WOW, this is a biggie! The food is fantastic; I'm cooking and chopping veggies, grains, nuts, etc. with more diversity than ever! I'm not supporting the deleterious meat and dairy industries, I don't have to take pharmaceuticals!

I am still learning and loving every minute. It has made me take a look at things that I never knew existed. Deep down, I get the satisfaction, with every single bite, I know I'm doing the right thing. I love all my new friends, that deep connection with the animals is something that...We Just Get It...and [it] keeps us together.

What are your favorite places to eat out in Portland?

Without a doubt, Blossoming Lotus.

What advice do you have for people going vegan?

Take it one step at a time, it can become overwhelming, seek out new friends that will help you along the way. Educate yourself. Think about the animals. Learn to cook.

Annual Vegan Events

Try Vegan New Year's Resolution:
When: January
An event designed to support transitioning vegans wanting to make a new year's resolution to become vegan.

Event features:
- Mentor meet-up
- Veganism 101 Q&A
- Food Fight Product Tour
- Guide to vegan cookbooks presented by Herbivore
- A good excuse to eat a cookie from Sweetpea Vegan Bakery

Activist Roundup:
When: January
A yearly gathering of non-profit organizations at Portland's all vegan mini-mall. Different organizations table and offer a chance for people to find out about various volunteer opportunities and local activist events. Groups ranging from animal rescues to animal activism organizations such as ADL and IDA.

Event features:
- Tables by various non-profit organizations
- Volunteer Opportunities
- Product Samples
- Something to do on a lonely, cold winter night. What else you gonna do?

Let Live Conference:
When: June
Animals belong to themselves, not to us. They should not suffer in our systems of food, science, entertainment and fashion. Instead, they should live free of the tyranny we put upon them. But they cannot claim this freedom alone. The Let Live NW Animal Rights Conference is a grassroots forum for people who want to help. Through an open, respectful, and friendly environment this conference will provide an opportunity for attendees to learn skills and strategies to become better advocates for the animals, regardless of one's experience level in activism.

This conference is for first-timers, experienced activists, and anybody in between who hopes to make a real difference for animals and build a stronger, more effective community and animal liberation movement. This conference is for anybody who wants to live and let live.

Event features:
- Educational Forum
- National Speakers
- Workshops
- Panel Discussions
- Food!
- Karaoke

Try Vegan Week:
When: August
Try Vegan Week is a weeklong vegan mentoring event that offers workshops, classes, store tours, bike rallies, and ends in a fun, fabulous Vegan Prom. Whether you have only recently come to the decision to live a cruelty-free life, or have been vegan for many years, Try Vegan PDX needs your support. Please tell your friends and get involved.

Event Features:
- Cooking Classes
- Educational Forums
- Potlucks
- Vegan Product Store Tours
- Movie Screenings
- Vegan Mentoring Meet-Ups
- Vegan Prom

VegFest:
When: September
VegFest celebrates and promotes sustainable, compassionate and healthy food choices and lifestyles. This low-cost, fun event welcomes everyone; with our uplifting atmosphere and positive approach to nurturing the world and building community, VegFest connects organizations, businesses and educators with the local public. In 2009, Northwest VEG will celebrate 5 years of VegFest, Portland's largest vegetarian festival!

Event Features:
- Notable speakers, experts and authors to discuss topics in health and nutrition, environmentalism, and animal welfare and compassion
- Food exhibitors/product sampling
- Exhibitor sales, including restaurant area
- Classes and workshops for easy entry to a healthy plant-based diet
- Chef demos
- Bookstore
- Family Activities
- Veg Lifestyle Product and Services exhibitors
- Non-profit organization exhibitors

Food Fight Anniversary:
When: September

Biggest vegan party of the year in Portland! Once a year vegan hipsters and crusties unite for a day of celebration to mark the anniversary of the coolest grocery store in the entire world. You can see videos and photos all over the Internet. Certainly not an event to miss!

Event Features
- Eating contests
- Velcro Walls
- Karaoke
- Free Food!
- Music
- Dancing
- All Out Good Time

Fur Free Friday:
When: November (Friday after Thanksgiving)

Fur-Free Friday is an annual event aimed at educating people about the horrors suffered by fur-bearing animals. Organized originally in 1986 by grassroots activists to abolish the fur trade, Fur-Free Friday has grown to be one of the most widely attended annual demonstrations of the animal rights movement. Through protests, education, and the promotion of cruelty-free fashion, LCA gives a voice to the millions of animals who suffer and die each year.

Event features:
- Speakers
- Rally & March
- Cheers by the Radical Cheerleaders for Animal Rights

Get Some Greens!

by Brian Heck of Sip

I must preface this article with a confession: I use to eat Tofurky Italian Sausages cold, straight out of the package; make vegan "meat-lovers" pizza on a weekly basis; and would rather slam my hand in a car door than eat a salad. Then, after about 8 years of not eating animals, it clicked: vegetables are *awesome*! Hindsight being 20/20, let me spare you and your GI tract the gut rot, nuclear farts, and food comas that come with the vegan faux meats and sweets diet. Don't get me wrong, fake meat and vegan doughnuts serve a their purpose, but they shouldn't be the mainstay of our diets.

Eat more greens!
Even if you don't fall into the aforementioned category, even if you're one of the healthiest people you know, even if you're raw, you could still use some more greens in your diet. The best way to eat more greens is actually to drink them. Over the past year, I've really fallen head over heels for greens, especially in liquid form. Green smoothies are a great way to trick your taste buds into thinking you're drinking a lovely fruit smoothie while giving your body the raw greens it's been screaming for. I know people who avoided vegetables like the plague, who now can't imagine going a day without a glass of the green stuff.

Drinking green smoothies makes you crave less crap, period. Once your body is really getting all its nutritional needs met, it stops craving a lot of the unhealthy foods. You no longer need the refined sugars and carbs in that breakfast muffin or the cheap high from your coffee. You'll actually find yourself starting to crave healthy whole foods instead. The main thing that makes green smoothies so great is they do the first part of digestion--chewing--better than you ever could. Most of the best nutrients in greens are found in their tough cell walls, which need to be ruptured in order for us to properly absorb the nutrients. Animals in nature will chew their greens to a creamy consistency before swallowing, something us human have neither the teeth nor patience for. Insert blender here. You could literally take a salad you were about to eat, throw it into a blender with a touch of water, and drink it. Not only would you get a lot more nutrition out of it, but you would have more energy, because your body didn't have to work as hard to digest it.

Digestion takes a lot of energy, so the easier foods are for our bodies to digest, the more energy we have to use on things like jumping rope or running from the cops. If your body's nutritional needs aren't being met, it needs to prioritize. When we're only providing enough energy and nutrients for day-to-day function, there's not a lot of room for maintenance and repairs, and we start to fall apart just like an old car. Our bodies are miraculous at healing themselves, but only if they have the tools to do so. The health advantages to drinking green smoothies have been attributed to curing a wide variety of ailments, including cancer, arthritis, diabetes, eczema and other skin related issues, not to mention greatly increasing energy and making us feel like a million bucks.

But what about my protein? Although you may not think of greens as having a lot of protein, they're actually a great source of it. Greens contain all eight essential amino acids, which are the building blocks your body uses to make protein. Whenever we eat protein, our bodies need to take it from the form that it's in, break it down into the 8 essential amino acids, and rebuild it as protein our bodies can use. If our bodies can start with the core ingredients for protein, we can skip the whole first step of breaking the protein down, and we're a lot more likely to absorb more of it. Just take a look at a cow or gorilla. They're enormous piles of muscle that sit around eating grass and leaves all day.

Here's a very simple formula you can follow to make yourself all the delicious green smoothies your mind can conjure up: 60% fruit, 40% greens. It's that easy.

Heres a recipe I like:

Sip's Greensicle:

. couple leaves of kale
. handful of spinach
. 1 banana
. 2 oranges
. vanilla extract

Toss all ingredients in a blender with a little ice and blend to a smooth consistency (making green smoothies is much easier a Vita-Mix or other high-powered blender, but one isn't necessary). If you're brand new to green smoothies, adding a little agave will instantly make them awesome. Eventually, you'll find yourself skipping the agave, and soon enough you'll be slamming handfuls of greens in your blender with just enough fruit and liquid to get them to spin. If you don't feel like making green smoothies yourself, stop by Sip, the adorable juice cart in front of Peoples Co-op, and they'll whip one up for you in no time. As vegans, we need to wean ourselves out of the deep-fried comfort food and binge doughnut-eating habits that seem to be prevailing as fake meat products and veganism become more mainstream. Vegan doughnuts are great, but they should be a treat, not a lifestyle. Skip the fake philly cheese steak tomorrow, go to the farmers market, buy some nice greens and fruit off your local farmers, and jam them into your blender. You'll feel awesome on so many levels. I promise.

For more information about green smoothies, check out the book "Green For Life" by Victoria Boutenko

Sip Milkshake Cart is located just outside People's Co-Op. Stop by and say hello to Brian sometime!

Vegan Parenting

By now you might be convinced that veganism is right for you, but what about your kids? Most parents' first concern is likely to be, "Is a vegan diet healthy for a child? Will a growing body be able to get all the nutrients it needs without animal products?" According to the experts, the answer to both those questions is unequivocally yes. In a statement published in 1998, the American Academy of Pediatrics Committee on Nutrition asserts that "well-planned vegan and vegetarian diets can satisfy the nutritional needs and promote normal growth of infants and young children." Even Dr. Spock (the pediatrician, not the Vulcan!) now recommends feeding children a vegan diet.

But how to convince the in-laws that this is a good idea? Your best bet is to educate yourself. Read as much as you can about vegan nutrition for children in order to arm yourself against any attacks from friends and loved ones. Also be sure that you can clearly articulate the reasons why veganism is important to you. There are also many places to get help with these explanations. The internet is full of information by and for vegan parents. Veganfamily.co.uk is a particularly helpful site run by a vegan family in Scotland. It includes information about nutrition, recipe ideas, tips for coping with various social situations, links to other helpful sites, and pages written by the family's two children, now teenagers, who went vegan with their parents as preschoolers. The book *Raising Vegan Children in a Non-Vegan World: A Complete Guide for Parents*, by Erin Pavlina, comes highly recommended for its practical advice on the day-to-day issues involved in vegan parenting.

So, what do vegan children eat? Breast milk from a well-nourished vegan mother is, of course, an ideal food for infants (and yes, it is vegan). However, if breast feeding is not desired or possible, vegan infant formulas are available commercially. Babies' first solid foods are usually things like rice cereal and pureed vegetables and fruits, which are vegan anyway. As children get older, they can begin to eat many of the same foods as their parents. It is also worth noting that vegan analogs to many traditional "kid foods" exist, although most of them shouldn't necessarily be eaten very often. Any supermarket with a decent natural foods section is likely to carry several different brands of vegan hot dogs and burgers, "chicken" nuggets, ice cream, cookies, frozen waffles, and so on. If that won't cut it, a trip to a food co-op, natural foods store, or Food Fight can allow you to stock up on vegan kid treats you wouldn't have dreamed existed, like Eco-Planet "cheese" crackers, Road's End Macaroni and Chreeze (it comes in a box with a packet of orange powder, just like a certain other non-vegan brand!), and marshmallows.

But nutrition, while important, is not the only consideration in deciding to raise children vegan. Brian McCarthy, the author of *The Vegan Family Cookbook*, emphasizes that kids usually just want to fit in, and offers suggestions to make that easier for vegan children. He advises parents to pack their children a school lunch that looks like those of their peers; for example, no one in an elementary school cafeteria would think twice about a child's eating a vegan lunch of peanut butter and jelly, carrot sticks, a juice box, and a (vegan) cookie. He also advises occasionally allowing children to eat vegan versions of the same kinds of "kid food" treats that they see their friends eating.

Stickier situations for children and their parents include school parties. McCarthy advises supplying enough of a vegan party food for the whole class. Other parents and teachers recommend sending in a supply of vegan treats that the teacher can store--cupcakes freeze well--and give to your child on days when others are celebrating. An advantage of that approach is that often even the teacher doesn't know ahead of time when someone will bring birthday cupcakes to school; if your treats are already there, you will always be prepared.

If children are invited to a play-date at a friend's house, McCarthy's advice is simply to schedule the date around mealtimes. If that isn't possible, try explaining your diet to the other child's family, and teach your child to say "no thank you" politely when someone passes her the steak. And try to resist the urge to quiz your child on what she ate the instant she returns to your home; instead, accept the possibility that she may have been less diligent than you would be about reading ingredients, or succumbed to temptation, and, in a relaxed way, help her learn what foods she should avoid in the future.

When children are invited to a birthday or other party, McCarthy, veganfamily.co.uk, and others feel that your best bet is to speak to the hosts ahead of time. That way you can explain your child's diet, and also find out what foods that will be served at the party so you can match them as closely as possible with a vegan alternative. It also helps if you send enough to share, so that your child isn't singled out as the one eating the "weird food."

One final piece of advice that all vegan parents seem to agree on: Be prepared! Keep a stash of snacks handy to avoid a cranky, hungry child meltdown when there's nary a vegan bite in sight.

Restaurant Guide

Price Guide:
$ - Entrees under $8
$$ - Entrees $8-12
$$$ - Entrees over $12

Veg-Friendly Guide
V - Vegetarian
V* - Vegan

NE Portland Restaurant Guide

Aladdin's Café - $$
6310 NE 33rd Avenue
503-546-7686
www.aladdinscafe.com
Recommended Dish: Vegetarian Mazza Combination

Arabian Breeze -$$
3223 NE Broadway
503-445-4700
www.arabianbreezeportland.com
Recommended Dish: Fatoush Salad, Falafel Sandwich

Bella Faccia - $ to $$
2934 NE Alberta Street
503-282-0600
www.bellafacciapizzeria.com
Recommended Dish: Vegan Pizza Slice

Black Sheep Bakery - $
523 NE 19th Avenue
503-517-5762
www.blacksheepbakery.com
Recommended Dish: Vegan Muffin or Bagel Sandwich

Blossoming Lotus – Irvington (V*) - $$$
1713 NE 15th Avenue
503-228-0048
www.blpdx.com
Recommended Dish: Daily Special

69

Blue Moose Café (V) - $ to $$
4936 NE Fremont Street
503-548-4475
Recommended Dish: Breakfast Burrito

Burritos Funny (cart) - $
E Burnside and 60th Avenue
Recommended Dish: Vegan Burrito

Bye and Bye (V*) - $$
1011 NE Alberta Street
503-281-0537
www.myspace.com/byeandbyeportland
Recommended Dish: Vegan Meatball Sub

Café Lucha (V*) – $
5420 E Burnside
503-995-9331
Recommended Dish: Bagel Sandwiches

Cup & Saucer Café - $ to $$
3000 NE Killingsworth Street
503-287-4427
www.cupandsaucercafe.com
Recommended Dish: Garden Scramble with Vegan Cheese

Dove Vivi Pizza - $ to $$
2727 NE Glisan Street
503-239-4444
www.dovevivipizza.com
Recommended Dish: Corn Cashew Vegan Pizza

Fuel Café - $
1452 NE Alberta Street
503-335-3835
Recommended Dish: Basil Vegan Sandwich

Grilled Cheese Grill (cart) - $
1027 NE Alberta Street
www.grilledcheesegrill.com
Recommended Dish: Vegan Grilled Cheese with Tomatoes

Homegrown Smoker BBQ (cart) (V*) - $
NE Alberta Street and NE 23rd Avenue
homegrownsmoker.wordpress.com
Recommended Dish: Smoked Soy Curls, BBQ Tempeh, Mac &
Cheese, BBQ Baked Beans

Horn of Africa - $ to $$
5237 NE Martin Luther King Jr. Blvd
503-331-9844
www.hornofafrica.net
Recommended Dish: Vegan Family Circle Platter

La Bonita Taqueria - $
2839 NE Alberta Street
503-281-3662
Recommended Dish: Veggie Burrito (no cheese, no sour cream)

LaurelThirst Public House - $
2958 NE Glisan Street
503-232-1504
www.laurelthirst.com
Recommended Dish: Vegan Pancake with Banana and Blueberries

Mash Tun Brew Pub - $$
2204 NE Alberta Street
503-548-4491
Recommended Dish: Vegan Veggie Burger

Prasad Cuisine (cart) (V) - $
NE Alberta Street between 14th and 15th
prasadcuisine.squarespace.com
Recommended Dish: TLTA Sandwich, Fresh Juices and Smoothies

Queen of Sheba - $$
2413 NE Martin Luther King Jr. Blvd
503-287-6302
www.queenofsheba.biz
Recommended Dish: Vegan Combo Platter

Spud Locker (cart) - $
NE 27th Avenue and NE Alberta Street
Recommended Dish: Patrol Boat Potato with Vegan Topping

Tour De Crepes (cart) – $ to $$
2921 NE Alberta Street
503-473-8657
www.tourdecrepes.blogspot.com
Recommended Dish: Vegan Crepe with Raspberries and Vegan
Chocolate

Vita Café - $ to $$
3023 NE Alberta Street
503-335-8233
www.vita-cafe.com

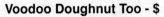

Try Vegan Week
Sponsor

Recommended Dish: Seitan Cheese Steak with Vegan
Cheese

Voodoo Doughnut Too - $
1501 NE Davis
503-235-2666
www.voodoodoughnut.com
Recommended: Vegan Apple Fritter, Vegan Portland Cream, Vegan
Voodoo Doll

Vegan Business Owner Profile:
Lisa Higgins - Sweetpea Bakery

How long have you been vegan and what turned you on to it originally?

I have been vegan for about 6 years now, I think. My friend Matt Simpson is probably the biggest influence on why I became vegan, he taught me a lot.

Sweetpea has evolved from a bakery selling to health stores to a full-blown cafe. What types of things can someone find at Sweetpea?

We make basic bakery items, like cakes, cupcakes and cookies, as well as pastries and doughnuts. We also serve some savory food, such as sandwiches, soups, and a daily bowl featuring a grain, bean and green.

You get a lot of non-vegan foot traffic. People are probably pretty surprised at how good your stuff tastes. What are the items that most often knock people's socks off?

Our most popular items are charlie browns (a chocolate peanut butter bar); our Saturday doughnuts; and our gluten, soy and sugar free muffin, called a nothin' muffin.

What are your favorite things about being vegan in Portland?

Obviously the endless food options, but also not having to explain what vegan is to everyone. People here already know!

Do you do parties and wedding cakes?

Yes, we do all kinds of special event cakes.

SE Portland Restaurant Guide

Aalto Lounge - $
3356 SE Belmont St
503-235-6041

Basement Pub - $
1028 SE 12th Ave
503-231-6068
www.basementpub.com

Bay Leaf Restaurant (V) - $$
4768 SE Division Street
503-232-7058
www.bayleafvegetarian.com
Recommended Dish: Eggplant Crisps

Bete-Lukas Ethiopian Restaurant - $ to $$
2504 SE 50th Ave, STE D
503-477-8778
www.bete-lukas.com

Black Sheep Bakery - $
833 SE Main Street
503-473-8534
www.blacksheepbakery.com
Recommended Dish: Vegan Muffin or Bagel Sandwich

Blue Monk - $$$
3341 SE Belmont Street
503-595-0575
www.thebluemonk.com
Recommended Dish: Vegan Lasagna

Bob's Red Mill Whole Grain Store & Cafe - $$
5000 SE International Way, Milwaukie, OR
503-607-6455
www.bobsredmill.com
Recommended Dish: Vegan Tofu Scrambler

Cellar Door Coffee - $
2001 SE 11th Avenue
503-234-7155
www.cellardoorcoffee.com
Recommended Dish: House Brewed Coffee

Chaos Café (V) - $ to $$
2620 SE Powell Blvd
503-546-8112
www.myspace.com/chaoscafe
Recommended Dish: The Lone Ranger

Cup & Saucer Café - $ to $$
3566 SE Hawthorne Blvd
503-236-6001
www.cupandsaucercafe.com
Recommended Dish: Garden Scramble with Vegan Cheese

Dots Café - $ to $$
2521 SE Clinton Street
503-235-0203
Recommended Dish: Spicy Fries with Tofu Dipping Sauce

El Brasero (cart) - $
SE 12th Avenue and SE Hawthorne Blvd
Recommended Dish: Soyrizo Burrito

El Nutri Taco (cart) - $
8438 SE Woodstock
Recommended Dish: Vegan Torta

Fat Kitty Falafel (cart) - $
2016 SE Division Street
Recommended Dish: Falafel

Fat Straw - $
4258 SE Hawthorne Blvd
503-233-3369
Recommended Dish: Bagel Sandwich and Bubble Tea with Coconut
Milk

Hammy's Pizza - $$
2114 SE Clinton St
503-235-1035
www.hammyspizza.com

Hoda's Middle Eastern Cuisine - $$
3401 SE Belmont Street
503-236-8325
www.hodas.com
Recommended Dish: Falafel Sandwich

Hungry Tiger Too - $ to $$
207 SE 12th Avenue
503-238-4321
www.myspace.com/hungrytigertoo
Recommended Dish: Portland Scramble with Vegan
Pancake or $1 Vegan Corndog Wednesdays

Try Vegan Week
Sponsor

India 4 U (V) - $$
3649 SE Belmont Street
503-239-8000

India Oven - $$
3450 SE Belmont Street
503-872-9687
Recommended Dish: Aloo Tikka

Iron Horse Restaurant - $$ to $$$
6034 SE Milwaukie Avenue
503-232-1826
www.portlandironhorse.com
Recommended Dish: Vegetable Chimichanga (ask for no dairy)

It's a Beautiful Pizza - $$
3342 SE Belmont Street
503-233-5444
www.beautifulpizza.com
Recommended Dish: Pizza with Pesto Sauce, Vegan Cheese,
Spinach, Black Olives & Sundried Tomatoes

Jam on Hawthorne - $ to $$
2239 SE Hawthorne Blvd
503-234-4790
Recommended Dish: Vegan Tofu Scramble with House Spices or
Vegan Chai Blueberry Pancakes

Jarra's Ethiopian & Langano Lounge - $$

1435 SE Hawthorne Blvd
503-230-8990
www.myspace.com/langanolounge
Recommended Dish: Vegan Combo Platter

Junior's Café - $ to $$
1742 SE 12th Avenue
503-467-4971
Recommended Dish: Vegan Tofu Scramble or Vegan French Toast

La Villa - $$
719 SE Morrison Street
503-872-9696

Langano Lounge
1435 SE Hawthorne Blvd
503-230-8990
www.myspace.com/langanolounge

Laughing Planet Café (Belmont) - $ to $$
3320 SE Belmont Street
503-235-6472
www.laughingplanetcafe.com
Recommended Dish: Che Guevara Burrito

Laughing Planet Café (Woodstock) - $ to $$
4110 SE Woodstock Blvd
503-788-2921
www.laughingplanetcafe.com
Recommended Dish: Cuban Bowl

Los Gorditos II (cart) (V*) - $
SE 8th Avenue and SE Ankeny
Recommended Dish: Vegan Torta, Tofu Burrito, Soyrizo Burrito

Nicholas Restaurant - $$
318 SE Grand Avenue
503-235-5123
www.nicholasrestaurant.com
Recommended Dish: Vegetarian Mezza (ask for it to be made
vegan) or Falafel Sandwich with Tahini

Oasis Café - $$
3701 SE Hawthorne Blvd
503-231-0901
http://www.oasispizza.com
Recommended Dish: The Elf Pizza

Old Wives' Tales - $$ to $$$
1300 E Burnside
503-238-0470
www.oldwivestalesrestaurant.com
Recommended Dish: Ask your server about vegan specials

Pad Thai Kitchen - $$
2309 SE Belmont Street
503-232-8766
Recommended Dish: Drunken Noodles with Tofu or Sweet and Sour
with Tofu (indicate strict vegetarian for all dishes)

Papa G's Deli (V*) - $$ to $$$
2314 SE Division Street
503-235-0244
www.pappags.com
Recommended Dish: Salad Bar

Paradox Palace Café - $ to $$
3439 SE Belmont Street
503-232-7508
www.paradoxorganiccafe.com
Recommended Dish: Vegan French Toast, Paradox Benedict, or
Solstice Corn Cakes

Perriera Creperie (cart) - $
SE 12th Avenue and SE Hawthorne Blvd
Recommended Dish: Vegan Crepe Special

Portobello Vegan Trattoria (V*) - $$ to $$$
2001 SE 11th Avenue
503-754-5993
www.portobellopdx.com
Recommended Dish: Potato Gnocchi and Tiramisu

Potato Champion! (cart) - $
SE 12th Avenue and SE Hawthorne Blvd
www.potatochampion.com
Recommended Dish: Belgian Fries with Rosemary Truffle Ketchup,
Vegan Poutine

Q BBQ (cart) - $
SE 12th Avenue and SE Hawthorne Blvd
Recommended Dish: Tofu Nuggets

Red & Black Café (V*) - $
400 SE 12th Avenue
503-231-3899
www.redandblackcafe.com
Recommended Dish: Dragon Noodle Bowl with Ginger Tofu

Report Lounge
1101 E Burnside St
503-236-6133
www.myspace.com/reportpdx

Sip (cart) (V*) - $
3029 SE 21st Avenue
www.myspace.com/getyoursipon
Recommended Dish: Milkshakes - Chocolate Peanut Butter, Cookies
& Cream, or Creamsicle

SweetPea Baking Company (V*) - $ to $$
1205 SE Stark Street
503-477-5916
www.sweetpeabaking.com
Recommended Dish: Sunday Brunch Buffet, Happy Bowls, Monster
Cookies

Tao of Tea (V)- $ to $$
3430 SE Belmont Street
503-736-0119
www.taooftea.com
Recommended Dish: Sweet Rice with Coconut and Mango

Taqueria Los Gorditos (cart) - $
SE 50th Avenue and SE Division Street
503-875-2615
Recommended Dish: Vegan Tofu Burrito or Soyrizo Burrito

Van Hahn (V) - $ to $$
8446 SE Division Street
503-788-0825
vanhanhrestaurant.com/default.aspx
Recommended Dish: Broccoli Combo

Vege Thai (V) - $ to $$
3272 SE Hawthorne Blvd
503-234-2171
www.vegethai.com
Recommended Dish: Pineapple Fried Rice (no egg)

Whiffies Fried Pies (cart) - $
SE 12th Avenue and SE Hawthorne Blvd
Recommended Dish: Vegan Chocolate Crème Pie, BBQ Tofu Pie

Whole Bowl (V) - $
4411 SE Hawthorne Blvd
503-757-2695
www.thewholebowl.com
Recommended Dish: The Whole Bowl (no cheese, no sour cream)

Wild Abandon - $$ to $$$
2411 SE Belmont Street
503-232-4458
www.wildabandonrestaurant.com

Ya Hala Restaurant - $$
8005 SE Stark Street
503-256-4484
www.yahalarestaurant.com
Recommended Dish: Veggie Mezza

Yarp?! (cart) - $
SE 12th Avenue and SW Hawthorne Blvd
Recommended Dish: Vegan Spaghetti with Veggies, Vegan Daily
Special

Vegan Business Owner Profile:
Grant Dixon - Papa G's

What does a vegan deli look like?

Well, we like to think it looks like a New York Jewish deli, just flesh free. Our main focus is on providing the freshest, best-tasting, highest quality food that you will find anywhere. We just believe that we have taken the meaning of "deli" to the next level by offering lots of raw foods as well as sandwiches, hot food, salads, soups and all of the other things that you are accustomed to finding at any quality deli.

We also think we take it to the next level by really using sustainable business practices. We use renewable power; we compost and recycle everything; we choose recycled and compostable paper, plastic, and to-go containers and products. We also used blue jean insulation and recycled paints in our remodel and have also used bamboo in tables and in many other applications, because it is a renewable resource.

We still feel like we are growing and learning ways for us to better serve our community with friendly service and all-organic food.

Why did you choose to make your deli 100% organic? Is it hard keeping strict?

We are 100% organic for the same reason that we are 100% vegan. We really believe that being a sustainable restaurant business requires us to use the fewest total resources. Animal products use an extremely large amount of resources, water, food, land, etc. Using non-organic food has a similar effect by poisoning the air, water, and land; not to mention the effects of the mono-crop system that is in place across much of the country that uses unknown amounts of future resources and causes unknown repercussions that are still to be realized. There is also the fact that large amounts of factory farming, as you know, are really inhumane and quite disgusting. Since I grew up on a family-run dairy farm I am really sad to see the industrialization of animals for food and their by-products. We are all-organic because we believe that to have the best tasting food, you should use the best ingredients.

There are really 2 elephants in the room when it comes to this discussion: the amount of resources we use to produce animal products, and the fact that most restaurants use a many extremely low-quality ingredients usually supplied by Sysco, Food Service of America, or Cash and Carry. Most of that food is made in China, most of it contains strange unpronounceable ingredients or corn by-products of some kind, and a lot of it isn't even properly labeled for items such as natural flavors that are meat/dairy based.

I really think that to be truly vegan, you have to be organic. It is not that hard to find organic versions of most ingredients these days, but the cost point is probably the hardest thing to deal with. Our food costs are lots higher than an average place's because of our commitment to organics. They're even higher than a lot of upscale spots' which, although they may be using local organic produce and meats, are still placing an order to the regular distributor for oils, grains, pastas, etc. We do really believe that there is a place in today's market and enough people out there who understand and care enough to spend the extra money to support these sustainable practices. However, we definitely get feedback that says we are too expensive although we are not even charging the normal restaurant/deli margins. We do understand that organic food is more expensive, and we hope not to turn those people away; we just tell them that their support us and our mission when they can is appreciated. Through more demand the cost always seems to decrease.

We feel like part of our mission has become to inform our customers and help them think about where their food is coming from and what the true cost really is. I don't want to be thought of as an elite spot, either. I really believe that people should grow more and more of their own food and feed themselves. We just want to be an option when they don't feel like cooking or are too busy. We think organic food should be available for all people. We are not like any other restaurant that exists today, since we are the only place that we know of that uses organic ingredients because of a true commitment to the cause, not just as a marketing tool to "greenwash" our place. The bottom line is that we believe in using REAL food with ingredients you can pronounce and recognize.

How long have you been vegan and what turned you on to it originally?

Papa G's has always been vegan since beginning in 1999. We started out selling our packaged tofu in local stores and did lots of festival vending and catering. I began working with vegetarian food in 1994 in Boulder, Colorado at a restaurant called Masala's. That is what really turned me onto the concept. That is when I began my journey into real food and started to learn about how our food was being modified. I then worked at the original Wild Oats Vegetarian Market, which really tied together the idea of vegetarian/vegan with natural foods.

I moved to Portland in 1996 and began working at the former Daily Grind, honing my skills in the kitchen and getting a great understanding not only of vegan food but also of allergen-free and natural foods.

Growing up we always had a huge fresh garden and what produce we didn't eat fresh was canned or frozen, so we never bought produce. So really, vegetables have always played a predominate role in my life.

What makes your salad bar so awesome?

We think that the fact that we make all of our deli salads from scratch, buy as much locally-grown fresh organic produce as is available, and think outside of the box when it comes to food really helps us create a salad bar that you don't see anywhere else! Right now we have fresh organic pineapple from Maui, local organic blueberries from Washington, local organic mixed greens [from] right here in Oregon, and Hijiki seaweed. Those are just a few of the kinds of ever-rotating items you will find on our salad bar, not to mention condiments galore and four house-made salad dressings. I don't know of anywhere else where you can find a salad bar with this quality and selection. We are also trying to do more sprouts and other items that are crucial to living a balanced, healthy lifestyle.

What are your favorite things about being vegan in Portland?

My favorite thing about vegan PDX is that there are so many options and such an understanding and acceptance of an alternative way of eating and living. I truly believe that only here, and generally on the west coast, are there enough people who get it as well as enough locally-grown resources and products for us to have a place that really is attempting to be truly sustainable and really is attempting to change the planet, one meal at a time.

Northwest VEG

For the Environment
For Your Health
For the Animals

www.nwveg.org

With your support, we promote plant-based diets & build community with:

- Monthly Portland potlucks
- Monthly dine-outs
- VegFest September 19, 2009
- Speaker Events
- Book Club
- Happy Hour
- Monthly Newsletter

- Master Vegetarian Program & Veg 101 Classes (Fall '09)
- Monthly Vancouver potlucks
- Veganic Gardening Group
- Valentine's Bake-off
- Compassionate Thanksgiving
- Outreach events and more!

Please join us as participants in our events and as a member.

Northwest VEG presents

Veg Fest

Portland Oregon 2009

Convention Center
September 19th, 10am–8pm

Vegfest features:
*Food Samples! *Speakers *Classes *Chef Demo's *Live Music
*Experts Table *Family Activities *Restaurants *Non-profits

Special Guests!
*Physician and Nutrition Expert, Dr. John McDougall
*Health and Wellness Expert, Kathy Freston
*Professional Athlete-Turned-Firefighter Rip Esselstyn

www.portlandvegfest.org

Vegan Business Owner Profile:
Aaron Adams - Portobello

What was the inspiration for your restaurant?

We're trying to bring together the aesthetic of casual fine dining, the ethics of using organic, locally sourced ingredients, and the accessibility of lower price. Plus, we wanted a venue to inform people about the plausibility of living a vegan lifestyle while being able to do fund raising for causes and organizations we care about.

What has been the biggest surprise of running Portobello?

How busy we've been has been my biggest surprise. I hoped to be busy, but in the back of mind I thought we'd maybe get only 20 people a night. Yeah for Portland for filling our dining room most every night. Another great surprise is how wonderful and thankful our customers have been. We have the greatest customers...our regulars are like family now.

What has been the reactions to the food from non-vegans?

We've had a great reception from non-vegans. A lot of vegans bring in their non-vegan friends and family. I remember one fellow who came in alone thinking it was a regular Italian joint. He was sort of upset at first, but ordered anyway, and had a great time. He stuck around for a while talking with us, and has been back since. Another standout was an ex-vegan from Spain who said he felt that he could give veganism a try again. That felt great.

What are your favorite things about being vegan Portland?

Accessibility. We truly are left wanting for nothing here in Portland. I am sure it will get better, too. I hear of new BBQ places, new pizza places...it's nuts. I always tell my friends who own vegan businesses, "We'll take this town block by block!" Seriously, I am all for more vegan restaurants in this town. There is plenty of room for it.

How long have you been vegan and what turned you on to it originally?

I was vegan when I was teenager (started in sixth grade as a vegetarian), then went away from it after cooking for a while. I was working in fine dining for over a decade, eating and serving meat and what not. I had a restaurant in Jacksonville, Florida, which served foie gras, veal, offals...everything horrible you can think of. One day I was sitting there thinking about it and freaked out. The short story is, I shut the restaurant down and headed back to the West Coast. I went vegan again (five years ago) and did some soul searching. After working some odd jobs, then as a machinist for a small pro bike tool manufacturer for a few years, my partner, Dinae, and I opened Portobello. It's hard work, but we're committed.

NW Portland Restaurant Guide

Andina Restaurant - $$$
1314 NW Glisan Street
503-228-9535
www.andinarestaurant.com
Recommended Dish: Ask your server for the Vegetarian/Vegan menu

Backspace (V) - $ to $$
115 NW 5th Avenue
503-248-2900
www.backspace.bz
Recommended Dish: Hummwich

Blossoming Lotus - Pearl (V*) - $$ to $$$
925 NW Davis Street
503-228-0048
www.blpdx.com
Recommended Dish: Daily Special and Vegan Soft Serve Ice Cream

**Chatpata Chaat Café & India Direct
Grocery (V) - $$**
16205 NW Bethany Court
503-690-0499
www.shopatindiadirect.com

Laughing Planet Café (21st Avenue) - $ to $$
922 NW 21st Avenue
503-445-1319
www.laughingplanetcafe.com
Recommended Dish: Che Guevara Burrito

Oba! - $$$
555 NW 12th Avenue
503-228-6161
www.obarestaurant.com

Someday Lounge (V) - $ to $$
125 NW 5th Avenue
503-248-1030
www.somedaylounge.com
Recommended Dish: Tempeh Reuben

Sweet Lemon Vegetarian Bistro (V) - $$ to $$$
4888 NW Bethany Blvd
503-617-1419
www.sweetlemonveggiebistro.com

The Tube Bar - $ to $$
18 NW 3rd Avenue
503-241-8823
www.myspace.com/tubeevents
Recommended Dish: Vegan Nachos

Vegetarian House (V) - $$ to $$$
22 NW 4th Avenue
503-274-0160
www.vegetarianhouse.com
Recommended Dish: Veggie Sweet and Sour Chicken

WORLDWIDE

STRONGEST

HELD
REAL VEGAN BELTS

SW Portland Restaurant Guide

Asaase Ital Palace (cart) - $
SW 5th Avenue and SW College
Recommended Dish: Golds & Greens Plate

Basha's (cart) - $
600 SW Pine Street
Recommended Dish: Spinach Pie

Bombay Chaat House (cart) - $
SW 12th Avenue and SW Yamhill Street
Recommended Dish: Vegan Lunch Special

DC Vegetarian (cart) (V) - $
SW 3rd Avenue and SW Stark Street

Divine Café (cart) (V) - $
SW 9th Avenue and SW Alder Street
503-314-9606

Down to Earth Café - $
7828 SW 35th Avenue
503-452-0196
www.downtoearthcafe.com

Dreamers Café (cart) (V) - $
SW 5th Avenue and SW Stark Street
Recommended Dish: Buffalo Tofu Wrap

Fernando's Mundo Fiesta (cart) - $
SW 4th Avenue and SW College
Recommended Dish: Vegan Wraps with Grilled Tofu

Food For Thought (V) - $
1825 SW Broadway
PSU Smith Memorial Student Union
503-725-9747
www.upa.pdx.edu/SP

Give Pizza a Chance (cart) - $ to $$
SW 5th Avenue and SW Stark Street
www.givepizzaachance.com/
Recommended Dish: Vegan Pizza or Vegan Calzone

Grandma Leeths - $$ to $$$
10122 SW Park Way
503-291-7800
www.grandmaleeths.com

Habibi - $$
1012 SW Morrison Street
503-274-0628
www.habibirestaurantpdx.com
Recommended Dish: Vegan Mezza

Huong's Pho (cart) - $
SW 10th Avenue between SW Alder and SW Washington
Recommended Dish: Vegan Pho

Hush Hush Café - $ to $$
433 SW 4th Avenue
503-274-1888
www.hushhushcafe.com
Recommended Dish: Vegetarian Meza Plate

India Chaat House (V) - $
804 SW 12th Avenue
503-241-7944
Recommended Dish: Vegan Lunch Special, Garlic Naan

Just Thai (cart) - $
SW 3rd Avenue and SW Stark Street
971-340-3011
justthaipdx.com
Recommended Dish: Vegan Pad Kee Mow

New Taste of India (cart) - $
1810 SW 4th Avenue *and* 340 SW 5th Avenue
503-888-0489 and 503-750-7435
Recommended Dish: Vegan Lunch Special

No Fish! Go Fish! (cart) - $
SW Yamhill Street and SW 5th Avenue
www.nofishgofish.com
Recommended Dish: Lunch Special with Vegan Soup & Black Olive,
Basil and Garlic Sandwiches

Persian House Restaurant - $$ to $$$
1026 SW Morrison Street
503-243-1430

Real Taste of India (cart) - $
111 SW 5th Avenue
Recommended Dish: Vegan Lunch Special

Savor Soup House (cart) - $
1003 SW Alder Street
www.savorsouphouse.com
Recommended Dish: Tomato Soup with Fennel and Orange

Shelly's Garden Burrito (cart) (V) - $
Pioneer Square (SW 6th Avenue and SW Morrison Street)
and SW Broadway and SW Yamhill St
www.honkinhuge.com
Recommended Dish: Honkin' Huge Burrito (non-dairy)

Swamp Shack (cart) - $
SW Stark Street and SW 5th Avenue
Recommended Dish: Vegan Jambalaya

Ugarit Mediterranean (cart) - $
SW 10th Avenue and SW Alder Street
Recommended Dish: Lentil Soup

Voodoo Doughnut - $
22 SW 3rd Avenue
503-241-4704
www.voodoodoughnut.com
Recommended Dish: Vegan Apple Fritter, Vegan Portland Cream,
Vegan Voodoo Doll

XV Bar - $ to $$
15 SW 2nd Avenue
503-790-9090
www.xvpdx.com
Recommended: Vegan Pizza and Sweet Potato Fries

Ziba's Pitas (cart) - $
SW 9th Avenue and SW Alder Street
Recommended Dish: Zucchini Pita

N Portland Restaurant Guide

Dalo's Kitchen - $$
4134 N Vancouver Avenue
503-808-9604
www.daloskitchen.com
Recommended Dish: Vegetable Platter

FlavourSpot (cart) - $
N Mississippi Avenue and N Fremont Street
and N Lombard between Denver and Greeley
flavourspot.com/
Recommended Dish: Vegan Sausage & Maple Waffle

Laughing Planet Café (Mississippi) - $ to $$
3765 N Mississippi Avenue
503-467-4146
www.laughingplanetcafe.com
Recommended Dish: Cuban Bowl

Pause - $ to $$
5101 N Interstate Ave
(971) 230-0705
Recommended Dish: Black Bean Burger

Pizza Fino - $ to $$
8225 N Denver Avenue
503-286-2100
www.pizzafino.com/
Recommended Dish: Vegan Pizza

Proper Eats Market & Café (V) - $ to $$
8638 N Lombard Avenue
503-445-2007
www.propereats.org
Recommended Dish: Daily Special, BBQ Tempeh Sandwich

Vendetta - $ to $$
4306 N Williams Avenue
503-288-1085
www.myspace.com/vendettapdx

Portland Vegan Profiles:
Isa Chandra Moskowitz - Cookbook Author

How long have you been vegan and what turned you on to it originally?

I actually went vegan about 20 years ago for the first time, but strayed for awhile as a lowly vegetarian. I eventually got myself together and went vegan again. I've always loved animals and so it was a natural choice for me. As any bumper sticker will tell you, it doesn't make sense to love [some] animals and eat others.

NYC is a fun place to be vegan - What drew you to Portland?

NY just became unlivable. I wanted a nice kitchen, more space for my cats, a garden. Plus, I thought I would hang out at the vegan mini-mall all day, twirl my hair and snap my gum.

What is your favorite thing about being vegan in Portland?

I love how normal veganism is here. So many restaurants have a vegan menu, or vegan icons to let us know what's vegan. Then there's just all the wonderful produce we've got.

How has writing cookbooks changed how you view advocating veganism?

I'm not sure that it has, sorry.

Advice for new vegans?

Don't stress and enjoy it. You've made the best decision of your life!

Other Vegan Businesses

Bicycle Shops

Veloshop
211 SW 9th Ave
503-335-VELO
www.veloshop.org

Clothing & Apparel

HELD Vegan Belts (V*)
503-804-4728
PDX, OR
http://m3house.org

Try Vegan Week
Sponsor

Herbivore Clothing (V*)
1211 SE Stark St
503-281-TOFU
www.herbivoreclothing.com

Pie Footwear
2916 NE Alberta St
503-288-1999

Try Vegan Week
Sponsor

Consulting and Education

Chef Al Chase, Consultant and Educator
503-752-2588
chefal@chefal.org

Donna Benjamin, Vegan Coach and Educator
503-752-2588
pdxvegan@gmail.com

Grocery, Co-op & Community Stores

Alberta Co-op
1500 NE Alberta St
503-287-4333
www.albertagrocery.coop

Food Fight! Vegan Grocery (V*)
217 SE Stark St
503-233-3910
www.foodfightgrocery.com

Food Front Co-op
2375 NW Thurman
503-222-5658
www.foodfront.coop

Limbo Inc (V)
4707 SE 39th Ave
Portland OR 97202

People's Co-op (V)
3029 SE 21st Ave
503-232-9051
www.peoples.coop
Note: While the store is completely vegetarian, the farmer's market occasionally sells meat.

Proper Eats Market & Café (V)
8638 N Lombard Ave
503-445-2007
www.propereats.org

Mirador Community Store
2106 SE Division St
503-231-5175
www.mirador-pdx.com

Hair Salons/Barbershops

Akemi Salon
3808 N Williams Ave, Ste D
503-542-5246
www.myspace.com/akemisalon

The Parlour
7327 N Charleston
503-289-0830

Stella's Barbershop
7540 N Interstate Ave
503-289-3868

Martial Arts Studios

Academy of Kung Fu
3228 SE 21st Ave
503-772-0600
www.academyofkungfu.org

Massage Studios

New Moon Massage Therapy (V*)
503-752-8340
www.myspace.com/newmoonmassage

Medical Groups/Physicians

Integrated Medicine Group
163 NE 102nd Ave, Bldg V
503-257-3327
www.integratedmedicinegroup.com

Naturopaths

John Collins ND
2907 Ne Weidler St
503-493-9155

Pet Supply Stores/Pet Groomers

Portland's Pampered Pets
4236 SE Hawthorne Blvd
503-233-2799

Publishers

Afterbirth Books
PO Box 6068
Lynnwood, WA 98036
www.afterbirthbooks.com

Try Vegan Week
Sponsor

Real Estate Agents

Adam Bartell
503-497-5367
www.adambartell.mywindermere.com/

Yvonne LeGrice
503-366-6776
www.yvonnelegrice.com

Tattoo Parlors

Adorn Body Art
9199 SW Beaverton-Hillsdale HWY
503-292-7060
www.adornbodyart.com
Note: Tattoo artist Jesse is vegan & uses vegan ink

Scapegoat Tattoo (V*)
1223 SE Stark St
503-232-4628
www.scapegoattattoo.com

Vegan or Activist Groups

NW Veg
503-224-7380
www.nwveg.org

Try Vegan Week
Sponsor

Portland Animal Defense League
www.pdxanimaldefense.com

Vegans for Animal Advocacy
503-725-9809
www.vegansforanimaladvocacy.com

NW In Defense of Animals (IDA)
5428 NE 30th Ave
503-249-9996
www.idausa.org

Farm Sanctuaries

Lighthouse Farm Sanctuary
www.lighthousefarmsanctuary.org

Out to Pasture Animal Sanctuary
503-756-8652
www.outtopasturesanctuary.org

Road Trips and Vegan Tourism

Although Portland has almost everything a vegan could want, it is also fun to travel around the Northwest. All of the major cities in our region have great vegan options. Here are a few of the highlights in each. If you're going on a trip it's best to check out local websites or happycow.net to get the full scoop.

This is not intended to be a complete guide of places to go and things to see; for that, consult a travel guide. We just want to help you find vegan grub!

Seattle

Seattle, WA is only a three-hour drive or a short train ride away. Portland and Seattle vegans like to argue over which city is more vegan-friendly, but just forget the debate and enjoy the food. Seattle has too many vegan-friendly options to list, but here are a few of the Try Vegan Team's favorites:

Bamboo Garden is an all-vegan Chinese restaurant in the shadow of the Space Needle. This menu, filled with mock-meat dishes, should please everyone--even your omni family members. (364 Roy St.)

Hillside Quickies is an all-vegan deli/sandwich and burger joint in Capitol Hill. It's short on seating but huge on flavor. The Venice Beach Veggie burger will blow your mind. (4106 Brooklyn Ave., Seattle; 324 15th Ave E., Seattle; and 1324 S. MLK Way,Tacoma)

Mighty-O Donuts sells only vegan, cake-style donuts in a huge variety of flavors. It's a great place to have breakfast. It's a little out of the way, but the experience is worth the trip. (2110 N. 55th St.)

Cinnamon Works: serves steaming hot cinnamon buns and cookies bigger than your face in the heart of Seattle's famous Pike Place market. The down side is Pike Place's vegan-unfriendliness, with its pervasive dead-fish odor and the risk of having a fish thrown at you! (1536 Pike Place).

Seattle's other great options include the all-vegan **Pizza Pi** (5500 University Way NE); **Wayward Cafe** (901 NE 55th St.), an all-vegan collective restaurant; **Squid and Ink** (1128 S. Albro st.), a greasy-spoon breakfast joint; **Teapot Vegetarian House** (125 15th Ave. E); and vegetarian hot dog place **Cyber Dogs** (909 Pike St.).

Eugene

Eugene is Oregon's second largest city, but it feels much more like a small college town than a big city. Eugene has become a hippie haven over the last decade or so and therefore has numerous vegan and veggie options.

Sweet Life Pâtisserie: This amazing bakery has lots to offer vegans with a sweet tooth. The offerings change daily, but wonderful cookies and cakes can always be found. They also have great brownies and other specialties. (755 Monroe St.)

Pizza Research Institute: The P^3 is a wonderful blend of pesto, pear and potato. Many people agree that it's not only the best vegan pizza they have ever had, but the best pizza they have ever had period. PRI has limited hours and is definitely a hippie paradise, but anyone who loves pizza will fit in just fine there. (520 Blair Blvd.)

Vancouver, BC

Canada's third-largest city is a scenic, five-hour drive north of Portland; a direct Portland-Vancouver train line is also in the works. Besides a great nightlife and gorgeous natural setting, Vancouver also boasts a number of excellent vegan and vegan-friendly restaurants.

The Naam: This all-vegetarian, largely-vegan diner is legendary for its vast menu and 24/7 service (closed on Christmas Day only). Enjoy the vegan pancakes and homemade "sausage" for breakfast! (2724 4th Ave. W)

Foundation Lounge: This funky, eclectic all-vegetarian eatery serves up huge portions of creative dishes at reasonable prices. Also, they have vegan fondue! (2301 Main St.)

Everybody Loves Veggies: This small, all-vegan eatery is just a food stall in a mall, but its "hippie fare" gets rave reviews. Simple, healthy, cheap, yummy vegan food with friendly service--what more could you ask for? (555 W 12th Ave.)

Victoria, BC

This beautiful Canadian city is on the southern coast of Vancouver Island in breathtaking British Columbia. Despite its small size, it has everything you could want in a city and is also close to amazing natural scenery. Victoria is accessible by ferry from Port Angeles, WA. After you get off the boat, you'll find several excellent tourist attractions like gardens, old-school fancy motels, year-round haunted houses, and bookstores. But let's talk about the food!

The Lotus Pond: All-vegan Buddhist Chinese restaurant, with a buffet-style lunch that is priced by the pound. It would put vegan bodybuilders in the poor house but is not too pricey for a reasonable amount of food. (617 Johnson St.)

Green Cuisine: Another all-vegan restaurant that sells entrées by the pound. The fries and baked goods are great. Different menu every day. Very healthy and tasty food. (5-560 Johnson St.)

The Joint: This pizza place is great, very vegan- and gluten-free-friendly. Get your pizza with Follow Your Heart vegan cheese and mock meats. Bonus: It's right next to the tattoo shop owned by Sarah Kramer, the author of the cookbook *How It All Vegan!* (1219 Wharf St.)

Lifestyles Market: The largest health food store in western Canada has all kinds of products we can't get in the States. Plus it's fun to read the ingredients in French. While the shopping is fun, be ready for the sticker shock. Remember that in BC they have national and provincial taxes, which we Americans sadly do not get that back in health care. (180-2950 Douglas St.)

Port Townsend

Stop by this little town on the Puget Sound on your way to Victoria. It has the best co-op or health food store west of Seattle (well, besides Lifestyles). There is also an entirely vegan and raw bed and breakfast/spa called Annapurna. There are several veg-friendly Thai and Indian restaurants, all of which are closed on Mondays. If you end up in PT on a Monday, try the tempeh mock tuna sammy at the co-op's deli, very yummy. Port Townsend can also be included on a trip from Seattle, since it is not far past Bainbridge Island.

San Francisco/Bay Area -

This is a longer trip but can still be done in a ten- to twelve-hour drive, or by Amtrak.

The Bay Area is a great veg-friendly region. Perhaps its only weakness is its lack of vegan breakfast options. Most of the vegan or raw restaurants have multiple locations around the Bay. Most vegan food connoisseurs will say that you must go to Millennium, which is San Fran's gourmet overpriced vegan foodie heaven. The authors of this article didn't go the last time we were in town, but they have a website and cookbooks so you can get a preview and decide whether you're willing to drop a fortune on their admittedly delicious food.

Herbivore: The best breakfast in the city, and a diverse all-vegan menu. Some highlights include savory crepes, pesto ravoli, and the swarma wrap. During our last trip to the Bay Area we ended up eating breakfast there twice. (531 Divisadero St., SF; 983 Valencia St., SF; 2451 Shattuck Ave., Berkeley)

Cha-Ya: All-vegan sushi and Japanese food. A huge variety of sushi rolls, noodle bowls, Tempura vegetables and more. The deep-fried portabella mushroom tempura stuffed with tofu is amazing. (762 Valencia St., SF; 1686 Shattuck Ave., Berkeley)

Maggie Mudd's: Although it's out of the way, a side trip to this vegan-friendly ice cream parlor is a must for the vegan with a sweet tooth. Banana sundaes, shakes, and cones are all served with homemade flavors of vegan ice cream. Don't miss this one. (903 Cortland Ave., SF)

Vegan Resource Guide

New to Portland and in need of some friends? Or new to veganism and in need of some friends who get it? Join Portland's vibrant vegan community by getting involved with some of these organizations:

NW Veg: The group that brings you VegFest also holds three potlucks a month in Portland and surrounding communities, regular dine-outs, a book club, and so much more. All activities are open to everyone, but membership gives you a discount at many local vegan and veg-friendly businesses. www.nwveg.org

Viva La Vegan: This group, based on Meetup.com, posts a wide variety of events including potlucks, happy hours, hikes, volunteer opportunities, classes, and anything else that seems fun! Tons of friendly people. www.meetup.com/viva-la-vegan/
Note: Meetup also has several other vegetarian, vegan, and raw-foods groups in the Portland area. This one is our favorite.

Try Vegan PDX: Okay, we're biased, but this is clearly the best organization around! Hook up with a mentor who can help you navigate the sometimes intimidating world of veganism. Or, if you're an experienced vegan, sign up to mentor someone else. Or just join us for year-round classes and events, not to mention Try Vegan Week and the Vegan Prom! www.tryveganpdx.com

In Defense of Animals (IDA): IDA is an international organization aimed at ending animal exploitation. Portland has a very active chapter that works hard to fight for animals' rights. Keep tabs on them at www.idausa.org; Food Fight's blog (www.foodfightgrocery.com) also often lists IDA events.

Let Live Foundation: Let Live runs an annual conference in Portland about veganism and animal rights, as well as a monthly talk or workshop. www.letlivefoundation.org

Other Helpful Resources:
Stumptown Vegans: www.stumptownvegans.com is an incredibly thorough listing of reviews of vegan-friendly restaurants in Portland and beyond. Complete with a searchable index.

Happy Cow: Lists vegetarian, vegan-friendly, and all-vegan restaurants in cities all over the world, and is therefore an invaluable tool when traveling. This link is to their Portland page: www.happycow.net/north_america/usa/oregon/portland/

LaVergne, TN USA
28 December 2009
168192LV00002B/3/P